J. Ernest Tinne

The Wonderland of the Antipodes

And Other Sketches of Travel in the Nisland of New Zealand

J. Ernest Tinne

The Wonderland of the Antipodes
And Other Sketches of Travel in the Nisland of New Zealand

ISBN/EAN: 9783744725309

Printed in Europe, USA, Canada, Australia, Japan

Cover: Foto ©Andreas Hilbeck / pixelio.de

More available books at **www.hansebooks.com**

THE

WONDERLAND OF THE ANTIPODES;

AND OTHER

SKETCHES OF TRAVEL

IN THE

NORTH ISLAND OF NEW ZEALAND.

BY

J. ERNEST TINNE, M.A.

(UNIVERSITY COLLEGE, OXFORD),
LATE EDITOR AND ORIGINATOR OF THE ETON COLLEGE CHRONICLE, AND
OXFORD UNDERGRADUATE'S JOURNAL.

WITH MAP AND NUMEROUS ILLUSTRATIONS BY THE AUTOTYPE PROCESS.

LONDON:
SAMPSON LOW, MARSTON, LOW, AND SEARLE,
CROWN BUILDINGS, 188, FLEET STREET.
1873.
[All Rights reserved.]

Dedicated

TO

MY FATHER,

WHO HAS DONE SO MUCH FOR ME; AND IN RETURN FOR WHOSE KIND AND CONSTANT AFFECTION, I HAVE BEEN AS YET UNABLE TO GIVE ANY BETTER PROOF OF MY GRATITUDE.

LIST OF PLATES.

	PAGE
Map of North Island of New Zealand	*Facing Titlepage.*
Roto-Mahana Lake ; General View, with Geysers	10
Te Tarata, or White Terrace	11
Te Tarata, and Geyser at Head	12
Basins of Te Tarata	13
Otukupuerangi, or Pink Terrace	14
Tattooed Basin—Te Tarata	15
Captain Mair and Arawa Native Constabulary, at Kaiteriria on Roto-kakahi	18
Ohinemutu on Rotorua, and Mokoia Island	19
Te Heu-Heu's Store-house—Lake Taupo	33
Bush Scenery, near Hokianga	51
Plan of Kaihu Estate	70
New Zealand Flax-bush (*Phormium Tenax*) near Hokianga	79
The Kawau—House and Bay	81
The Kawau—Sir George Grey's House and Garden	86

NEARLY all the recent writers on New Zealand, such as Lady Barker, Sir C. Dilke, and others, have confined themselves to the South or Middle island, where the people, climate, and imported trees remind one so strongly of England, that it is hard to imagine yourself away from home. But though the glaciers and lake scenery of the Southern Alps are in their way almost unrivalled, I think that for variety, beauty. and interest, the natural phenomena of the North island are pre-eminently wonderful; whilst the semi-tropical look of the vegetation, the influence, manners and customs of the Maori population, and the eternal spring weather, lend a powerful charm of novelty to visitors in these parts.

In 1872 I spent some time in exploring the celebrated Hot Lakes of Rotorua and Rotomahana, continuing my journey on horseback from thence to Lake Taupo and Napier; and as my experience tends strongly to confirm the impressions formed by the late Governor Sir G. Bowen, as to the peaceful disposition and hospitality of the natives in recently disaffected districts, I have no hesitation in trying to persuade sight-seers and *bond fide* emigrants to visit or adopt for their home the "Eden of the Southern Seas," without fear of any further serious disturbances. To the account of this expedition I have added several selected sketches of places and things not generally known, in preference to inflicting on the public a complete account of my travels or giving descriptions of what may have already been told in far more graphic language than mine pretends to be. I have borne in mind two maxims; firstly, that

Omne tulit punctum, qui miscuit utile dulci,

in accordance with which I have tried to combine useful guide-book information with personal incidents, and thus to dress the former in a more pleasing garb; secondly, that

Segnius irritant animam demissa per aurem
Quam quæ sunt oculis submissa fidelibus:

and therefore I have embellished the pages, where I could, with correct copies of photographs taken by Mr. Munday, of Wellington, and Mr. Möller, of Auckland, on the very spots of which I speak.

Mr. Anthony Trollope, in his recently published work on the colonies, mentions that four hundred books have already been written about New Zealand, but that as he never read one of them himself previous to his visit there, he ventures to think there may be room for just one more still. Being venturous enough to tread in his steps, I must plead the same excuse in presenting to the public number four hundred and two, which I feel assured is far from exhausting what may be said in praise of "the coming country."

THE WONDER-LAND OF THE ANTIPODES.

On one of those bright summer evenings in Auckland when the whole landscape is bathed in a luscious light which serves to intensify the beauty of the surrounding scenery, and bring out with wonderful distinctness the clear-cut outlines of the trees and mountains against a warm blue sky (unrivalled elsewhere in the world), I rode up the Grafton Road towards Mount Eden, where I was to spend the night with some hospitable friends, before starting on my journey overland to the Waikato Settlements, Hot Lakes, and Napier. My whole equipment was comprised in my horse, saddle and bridle, mackintosh, and a leathern valise weighing about fourteen pounds, which contained change of clothing, etc., and a small packet of plug tobacco for presents to the natives. With an exhilarating sense of freedom from care, and the anticipation of a pleasant companion to the end of my first stage at Hamilton, I felt thoroughly contented. I could not help gazing back at times on the lovely Waitemata harbour beneath me, with the extinct volcano of Rangitoto gracefully rising in the foreground, and far in the distance the purple ranges at Coromandel and the Thames, across which, though miles away, I could see my track lying over the Razor Back, like a white line on the side of the mountain. No one without actual experience of it can realize the life-giving buoyancy of the New Zealand and Tasmanian climates; they are "as cream to skim milk" compared with the atmosphere of our own little fog-bound island; so that the mere sense of existence, "breathing and having our being," is vividly delightful in these latitudes. These are lands from which, as a Californian said of his own country, "you must go away if you want to die." Then, too, a man feels so completely his own master on horseback (unless indeed the case be exactly reversed, and the horse be master of the man); he can stop when and where he likes, and watch the coach-passengers hasten away from a half-eaten, uncomfortable meal, with all that inward satisfaction which (selfish though it be) we really do feel when contemplating the misfortunes of others and prosperous ourselves. Leaving Mount Eden in the early morning, we struck into the Waikato road, stopping at Drury for dinner, and rode fifty-two miles that day to Rangirirei, where we saw the remains of the old pah or fortress, so celebrated during the last war with the Maories. I found myself rather saddle-sick with the effects of the first day's ride; but in a very short time became hardened with continual exercise, until fatigue and I were comparative strangers. As we cantered along the left bank of the Waikato, the pheasants, which have been acclimatised, and are now rapidly spreading over the island, kept rising in twenties and thirties at our horses' feet from the road, where they were feeding on the swarms of crickets; and we caught occasional glimpses on the other bank of flax-mills, with their snowy fibre drying on the fern; of the wild peach groves, for which Auckland province is so justly famed; of coal mines; and of native enclosures, with their little patches of tobacco, cumera (sweet potato), and maize. And before I forget it, I must here relate an amusing incident which took place *en route*. My horse, which had been very leg-weary at starting, and had pitched heavily on his head as we rode into Rangirirei at dusk, the previous evening, sending me head first among the manuka or ti-tree scrub, suddenly "gave out" to such an extent that I had to stop at an "accommodation house" (or way-side inn) to sponge him down. In course of conversation with the proprietor, I happened to mention that the poor beast had covered about two hundred miles in three days just before I got him, whilst the detectives were in search of a notorious convict named Robinson, who had recently escaped from Mount Eden gaol; the man slipped away into the house, and shortly afterwards, when I requested them to give me a "nobbler" or drink, his wife informed me that not having a spirit license, she must refuse to serve me; evidently mistaking me for one of the constabulary in disguise. It took a considerable amount of persuasion to convince her that I was no informer, but I eventually succeeded in obtaining what I wanted. On crossing the ferry at Ngaruawahia or Newcastle, where the Waipa joins the Waikato, we were a good deal interested while waiting for luncheon, with the primitive way in which the resident magistrate, who had joined us on the road, held his court on the verandah of the hotel. He had to decide a case of horse-stealing, or disputed ownership; the prisoner and accuser argued their own sides of the question, marching up and down the common in front of the house, with violent gesticulations as each in turn spoke, and occasionally throwing back the blanket from their shoulders as if about at once to settle the dispute *vi et armis*. "Much cry and little wool," however, for the decision once pronounced, the defeated individual quietly lay down, without a trace of excitement, and smoked himself into a comfortable doze.

I spent the night at Hamilton, a neat little town, situated on either side of the river; and devoted the next few days at Ohaupo, to observing the marvellous energy and rapidity with which settlers are transforming the dusky brown fern land of the surrounding country into the most charming dairy-farms and sheep-runs, with less labour and expense than is the case in any district I had before visited, except perhaps the virgin prairies of Kansas, which, however, cannot compare with this district for climate and scenery. I stayed for a time at the house of Mr. C——, a squatter, who has migrated hence from Canterbury, with whose son I had ridden up from Auckland, and who is largely engaged in reclaiming the vast swamp which lies between Ohaupo and Hamilton. Behind us rose the mountain of Pironghia, on the border of the "King's country," near which Todd, the road surveyor, was murdered by the rebels a year or two ago, whilst working well *within* the boundaries of the confiscated lands. It is a subject of regret with me that I did not visit Alexandra and Te Awamutu, which lie in that direction, as I have been since told that the homesteads there present even a more thoroughly English appearance, with their neat enclosures and country stiles, than the districts I rode through. Crossing the plain from Ohaupo to Cambridge, on a still close day, the notice of the traveller is attracted by the pillars of dust, exactly resembling a waterspout in appearance and shape, which rise at intervals in a whirlwind to the clouds, scud across the fields, and then as suddenly collapse. Shortly after arriving at the hotel, I made the acquaintance of Major Drummond Hay, whose amusing anecdotes and hair-breadth escapes by land and water enlivened an ever memorable evening. This gentleman told me that he had not seen his "young brother Frank," our Consul-General at Tripoli, for nearly twenty years; and as I myself had spent six months in that town, during 1870, to investigate the circumstances of the murder of Miss Tinne, the Dutch Traveller, and had been in pretty constant communication with the British Consulate, a bond of union was at once established between us in my African reminiscences. Among other bush-stories, some of which savoured a trifle of Munchausenism, one especially tickled my fancy. A "new chum," or novice in colonial life, was consulting my friend as to what amount of luggage he would advise for bush travel. "Well!" replied the Major, "I myself prefer to carry nothing but an empty canvass bag of moderate dimensions."

"What on earth is the good of that?" said his friend.

"If it rains," said the Major, "I immediately take off my clothing, place it in the bag, and walk on till it stops, when I am in the enviable position of having a dry suit to fall back on at the end of my journey."

I was just thinking of retiring to bed, when I heard a familiar voice in the adjoining room, and, looking in, found an Auckland man, Mr. M——, who was on his way to the Hot Lakes, in company with two friends from Australia. They invited me to join their party so far, and, as I had not yet secured a guide, I was glad to avail myself of their kindness. We appointed M. commissariat officer to the expedition, and it was chiefly owing to his prudence in catering, that we owed our successful journey; a verier desert for man or beast than the Lake district I never saw; the stores are nearly always empty, and beyond the mere necessaries of life, such as potatoes and bacon, literal starvation threatens the unwary traveller in these parts. We laid in a bountiful supply of sardines, canned salmon, jams, biscuits, tea, cocoa, and sugar; also a tin pannikin apiece, and a "billy" for boiling the water. Meanwhile I mounted my "bag of bones" and rode out to "Walker's Swamp" at Moana-tui-tui, to try and obtain a change of horses. I was fortunate enough to find a strong black mare, which, though slow, was in good condition, and likely to last me through to Napier. My visit to Mr. Walker was otherwise interesting, for he explained to me the curious history of his "swamp," which at first appeared to me a "lusus naturæ" from its height above the surrounding plain, and facilities for drainage. It seems that centuries ago, the Maories, who even now subsist to a large extent on eels and sharks' fins, had dammed up the stream running from this plateau, with a strong and wide barrier of ti-tree fascines, which I could still see at the bottom of the deep drain recently cut through the land; and having thus formed immense eel preserves in the soft mire, they left a very small opening in the centre of the dam, where they laid their wicker basket eel traps, and thus secured a regular supply of food. Rejoining my party, we made a late start for Maunga-tautari, the first halting-place, about twelve miles distant, where our guide lived, the only white man in the settlement. My English friends would have laughed to see us, after we had made up our beds of fern in the tents, sitting round the camp-fire with our new acquaintances, and subjected to their running fire of criticism and wit. Many of the women were suckling small pigs and puppies at their breasts, a disgusting habit, for which I can offer no reasonable explanation. The pigs do not always reciprocate the affection that is thus shown them, for we were informed that they had half-eaten an old Maori woman a week or two before, as she lay sick on the floor of her hut; and her friends, on returning from work, found her body in a shockingly mutilated condition. The women, after they have done smoking, have a nasty practice of sticking the pipe through the place where an earring ought to go, which disfigures the lobe of the ear immensely. Very often, by way of quieting their squalling babies, who are strapped on to their mothers' backs, you see them hand a half-finished pipe of tobacco to the child over their shoulder, who immediately stops his cries and sucks away with the utmost contentment. Fancy these *tamariki*, piccaninnies or brats of one or two years old, indulging thus early in the herb nicotiana. They were immensely delighted with some comic songs which I sang to them, and joined in the chorus of "When Johnny comes marching home again," with rather laughable pronunciation, but evidently a quick ear for music.

I was much pleased with one little trait of their good nature; they noticed that I was the only one of the party without a blanket, and, after peeping into the tent several times, a young girl pulled her new shawl off with a muttered ejaculation of pity, and threw it over me, running away immediately to nestle in the adjacent mass of Maori humanity round the fire, where I hope she found warmth enough to compensate for the loss of clothing. I rewarded her next morning with a plug of my best tobacco, which evidently more than repaid her for the loan of the shawl. In the grey dawn we saddled our steeds and reached the ferry, where we crossed in canoes, having previously swam the horses over under the leadership of one old "stager," who took to the water more like a duck than a quadruped. The morning's ride was rather uninteresting, over endless plains of tussock grass, and small but rapid streams of the purest water. We reached Te Whetu, a village of Hau-haus, or former rebels, very early in the afternoon, but decided to travel no further that day, as the sky had already become overcast, and we should have had to bivouac under a drenching downpour of rain, in lieu of enjoying dry and comfortable quarters at the great "whare-puna," or meeting-house, of the tribe. This building was a fine specimen of Maori architecture; the walls being formed of raupo or rushes laced together with flax, and fastened to the huge beams of totara, on which I noticed carvings more ingenious and grotesque than decent. We were treated here with the utmost hospitality; the old "rangatira," or gentleman-farmer and his wife who were in charge, made a mess of pottage, with chickens, onions, and potatoes, for which Esau would have sold his birth-right a second time; whilst they apologised with finished courtesy for not having a Union Jack to hoist on the flag-staff in honour of our arrival. This latter want we have since rectified, by sending them a flag from Auckland with which to welcome future travellers. Our journey on the following day was rather more exciting. After a precipitous descent of eight hundred feet from the Pass of Painuiorehua, down which the pack-horse, a one-eyed but sagacious beast, rather slid than walked, to the imminent risk of our "swags;" and, crossing a series of tantalizing swamps, at times glancing past an old geyser-hole within a few inches of the track, with its treacherous depths half concealed by an over-growth of lovely creeping ferns; drenched through and through with rain, αὐτοὶ ἀημενοὶ τε, we at last reached Kaiteriria, a pretty settlement on the shores of Roto-Kakahi, and found there the head quarters of Captain Mair, of the Arawa contingent of Native Constabulary, who gave us a hearty welcome, and in the evening invited us to visit him and inspect his rare collection of Maori curiosities, such as kiwi-feather capes; flax mats; tobacco-pipes carved from the ti-tree wood into quaint little figures with huge mother-of-pearl eyes, the work of a hunchback, named Bartholomew, from Opotiki on the East Coast, whose art has now become obsolete with his eyesight; and, lastly, the great Toutanikai's flute, made from a human thigh-bone, to which I shall refer later on in the legends of Rotorua.

Rotokākahi is "a very pretty lake, completely shut in

by precipitous but verdure-clad mountains, with the bright little island of Mōtu-tāwa, set like a jewel in the midst of its cold dark-blue waters." Here we spent a day to recruit our spent energies and dry our clothes, whilst the native lads strummed away on their Jew's harps, or danced the "haka" outside the door of the "wharé." We started hence too late to make Kariri and Tarawera Lake, and had to sleep in a hut at the old mission-station of Wairoa, where even Keating's Persian Insect Powder proved ineffectual to stay the appetite of certain unwelcome bed-fellows, which actively assailed us throughout the night. As there seemed to be a faint chance of our horses obtaining a bite of food about the settlement, and our oats were rapidly running short, we walked on next morning to Tarawera Lake, where we were to embark, and sat down on arrival to a repast of potatoes, apples, and cray-fish, which I thoroughly enjoyed. A difficulty now arose about manning the canoes, as the men were all absent road-making, and the women very naturally refused to leave their babies behind them alone. Finally, we arranged "to take the lot," and accordingly stowed away our own party of six, seven Maori women, a steersman, manifold children and dogs, and numerous kits of potatoes, into one large but somewhat leaky canoe. I shall never forget our paddle across Tarawera; the women, working like demons (their eyes rolling and tongues lolling), bursting ever and anon into a wild excited chorus of Hekaté-koraré-hekaté as we shot rapidly over the waves, towards the hot river which flows from Rotomahana, the gem par excellence of the whole volcanic district. This little lake is situated in the midst of the most astounding natural phenomena, each one of which would at once make any more civilised locality the Utopia of invalids and sight-seers. The tepid waters of the lake itself are the resort of innumerable water-fowl, which, however, are "tapu," or sacred from the gun of the sportsman, as they glide peacefully on the bosom of the waters, or scream defiance at the intruder on these fairy precincts—the wonder-land of the habitable world.

Landing at some dilapidated huts on the edge of the lake, we were soon luxuriating in the delights of a "waireka" (hot tank), the temperature of which may be regulated at pleasure by turning in boiling water from the neighbouring geyser, in which our pots of potatoes were being rapidly cooked; the natives warned us against laying our clothes on the ground, as the exhalations of vitriol rapidly destroy anything with which they are brought in contact. I spent a very restless night, for the whole surrounding country seems alive with escape-pipes of steam, and I could hear the grumble of the water at no very great distance beneath my head. I awoke in the morning with my clothes perfectly soaked by the vapour which rose from the holes in which the side-posts of the huts were fixed. In our immediate neighbourhood also we noticed that several wharés had completely sunk through the crust into the boiling mud, at no very recent date; and we shuddered as we thought of the possible fate of their poor inmates. We had a partial exemplification of this danger when on our way to the geysers, for one of my companions was imprudent enough to place his foot down, a few inches from the beaten track, and immediately began to sink into the scalding mud. He cried for assistance, and I caught him by the hand before any very serious injury was done; but on cutting off the boot we found his ancle and instep badly blistered, which incapacitated him from further exertions that day. A most vexatious incident to commence our explorations with!

The first sight of interest was Te Tarata or the White Terrace, a series or gradation of seven or eight most lovely

white basins, formed by a deposit of silica from the overflowings of the great geysers at the summit. The water itself is strongly sulphurous, and of the deepest azure blue; whilst the edges of each basin are adorned with the most delicate incrustation, almost resembling lace-work in its delicate regularity. We found several insects, such as grasshoppers and beetles, beautifully petrified; but were unable to bring away specimens owing to the brittleness of the substance, which would have involved more careful transport than we could give. The temperature and depth of the water vary considerably, as the wind backs up the overflow, or drives it down the face of the terrace.

As we picked our way across the Terrace, one of the old Maori women suddenly began to yell with fright at the increasing temperature of the water, which was beginning to penetrate the horny soles of her feet; so we had to make stepping-stones of ourselves till we got her to the edge again. Although she bitterly complained at first of her parboiled state, a small douceur proved a very efficacious cure, and she soon walked as soundly as the rest. Retracing our way past the wharé, where we had slept, and stopping here and there for the amusement of "chocking" a geyser-mouth with stones and lumps of earth, to see it suddenly burst thirty or forty feet into the air with redoubled vigour, we found ourselves on a large flat of pinkish mud, dotted at intervals with small cones, which kept spitting up clots of scalding liquid, about the consistency of thick cream. We picked our steps very cautiously to the head of the gully, and there found a large pool, called Roto Pounamu, or the Cold Green Lake, whose waters are tinged with some vegetable substance, which renders them of the deepest emerald hue. Further along this shore of the lake are other geysers and small terraces, whose name is Legion, each one differing slightly in appearance or flow, and each with some curious Maori legend attached. One large basin we saw, into which two babies had been thrown and cooked at a sacred feast, in the "good old cannibal days" of the country; and another into which a woman had fallen and disappeared. The "Babies' Cauldron" appeared to me well adapted for the purpose, as it was always at a uniform steady boil, and never rose into the air with a surging column of water, like the more turbulent ngahaus around. The water also was less impregnated with sulphur, and so would affect the flavour of the cookery less; it was green in colour, unlike the lovely blue of Te Tarata.

On taking to our canoe again, we paddled to the west side of the lake, and landed at the foot of Otukupuerangi, or the Pink Terrace, in which the basins are larger and better defined; but there is not quite so intricate a device of trace-work on the hard enamelled surface as in those of Te Tarata. To the right, as you ascend, is an immense boiling hole, almost on the lake-level, the yellow walls of which are composed of the purest flower of sulphur, and present a striking contrast to the pink and blue colouring of the adjacent terrace. Here we could no longer resist the temptation of a swim; and the luxury of that bathe I shall never forget. The water imparted a silkiness to the skin which no artificial nostrum can give; and the great delight of the whole affair to me was that Nature herself had here provided a lounge, with which the marble tanks of the ancients could not for a moment compare.

Did you require additional warmth, you had but to take a step up towards the great blue depths of the geyser, whence the water flowed down into successive basins, each more lovely than the other. Did you wish to brace your flagging powers from the enervating warmth of the sulphur-bath, with three or four bounds down the face of the

terrace you could take a final dive into the colder depths of Rotomahana, and return invigorated to the spotless ledge which formed your temporary dressing-room. I regret to notice that here, as everywhere, the pet vice of English travellers is predominant, and that an entire step of the terrace has been finally disfigured by the names (scribbled in pencil) of nearly every visitor to the place. So rapid is the coating or deposit from the waters, that the writing is now imperishable, and cannot be effaced without destroying the rock. Not only have the contemptible effusions of would-be poets been here immortalized, but eminent personages have thoughtlessly emblazoned their autographs side-by-side with the "nobodies," to whom this cheap means of notoriety is usually confined. We turned our backs on Rotomahana with regret, for it would be the study of a life-time to describe or discover *all* its marvels, and we had scarcely devoted one entire day to our visit. But it was a clear case of starve-out for our horses and ourselves, if we remained longer in the district; for all the stores seemed empty, the people away, and the promised supplies of oats — which are all "packed" from the coast, and frequently run short even in the summer season, when tourists abound — had now entirely failed us for a time; and, unless our poor beasts could at once change their habits, the fern, ti-tree, and tutu which monopolise the district would have proved but a sorry substitute for their natural diet.

Shooting the rapids at precipitous speed, and amid intense excitement of all but the old steersman, who sat immovably at the stern, like a tattooed statue in bronze, we were soon floating on the broad bosom of Tarawera. We landed in one of the little bays, and after mooring our canoes under the shade of some gigantic pohutakawas, whose knotted arms make the best possible "elbows and knees" for shipbuilders' work, we watched with some interest the preparation of our food in a genuine copu-maori, or native oven. This was done as follows: the women scraped a hole in the soft ground with their hands, and filled it with dry wood, to which they set a light. On the top of the blazing fire they placed stones about the size of a man's two fists, which became heated and dropped through as the fuel burnt out. Then having collected fish, potatoes, and a few squashes, which we found in the deserted settlement hard by, they brought a good-sized pannikin of fresh water, dashed it over the stones, and, before the steam had time to escape, filled the hole in with the provisions. On the top of these a clean kit, or handbag of woven native flax, was placed; then some armfuls of fresh-cut fern, and lastly a pretty thick layer of soft mould, which they patted down till there was no aperture by which the vapour could escape. In about twenty minutes the cooking was complete, and we sat down to a frugal but most delicious repast of steamed food, which I thought much superior to the usual boiled vegetables of an English cuisine. We coaxed some of the little children into friendship by letting them drink the oil from our sardine-tins when we had eaten the fish; but they evidently looked upon us as a kind of white-faced ogres, whom it was prudent to keep at a respectful distance. One little pickle of a fellow, with bright black eyes, who had quite overcome his terror, amused himself by creeping up behind the others, and frightening them by shouting in their ear, "Nui pakeha, nui pakeha" (the big white man, the big white man) "is coming"—meaning me; at which they would burst into tears, and run like rabbits from the supposed cannibal—your humble servant. They had evidently been taught the same cock-and-bull stories that English nurses often inflict on their charges, of the giants that eat naughty children, only that here the case was reversed, and instead of the "big black man" in the myths of our infancy, our pale-faces produced a similar effect on them.

We held a "drawing-room" at Kariri that evening, in a small hut of 8 feet by 18, with a small aperture (misnamed a door), through which I could scarcely drag myself even when prostrate. Imagine the state of the atmosphere, with a smoky fire of green wood, no chimney, and about twenty Maori ladies and children all smoking furiously at their pipes, and nearly a hundred-weight of green tobacco steaming on the walls preparatory to use!

I had heard a good deal of the fresh-water cray-fish (goura) that are found in these lakes, and asked whether I could have some of them. My wish was soon gratified, but my equanimity was a good deal disturbed, for when a kit of them was produced, instead of letting me shell them myself, an old hag, with very dirty fingers, seated herself opposite to me and proffered her services. A sense of etiquette forbade me to decline, so I screwed up my courage and held out a biscuit for her to lay the first slippery morsel upon. It went down pretty easily, and when she had given us two or three dozen, like the Greek travellers of old, "*mensas etiam consumpsimus*," we even ate our temporary plates as a finale to the repast.

I noticed several plots of tobacco in this settlement, with its pretty pink flowers; and from what I know of Tennessee and Virginia, I am confident "the noxious weed" would thrive exceptionally well in the North Island of New Zealand; the soil in places has the same bright red appearance here as in America, and the climate is bright, warm, and moist. At present, all that the natives raise is solely for their own use, but I live in hopes of seeing it become in the future a leading article of manufacture or

B

export. The Maori women are most persistent smokers, and when the pipe is off duty, as I have said before, it is stuck through the lobe of the ear in the place where the ear-ring ought to be, much as our clerks at home stick their pen behind their ears. The weight of the pipe, however, has occasionally the disagreeable effect of wearing the ear through, and making a piece drop off.

We were glad to "quit" early next day, and stopped for breakfast at the Wairoa, where old Mary, native servant to the missionary, Mr. Spencer, made a welcome contribution of fruit to our scanty breakfast. Thence, leaving Kaiteriria behind us, and passing on the left hand Tiki-tapu, or the Blue Lake, we entered a thick bush on the road to Rotorua. The scarlet rata was still in flower, and I succeeded in obtaining some bunches for my companions, to whom it was not familiar. This curious parasite is said to begin its growth in the branches of the tree to which it is found attached, gradually dropping downwards to the ground to obtain redoubled strength by its contact with mother earth, when it strangles its parent support in a deadly embrace.

A faint smell of brimstone, such as Mark Twain says would not be unpleasant to a sinner, met us while some miles from our destination, and ere long we sighted the native village of Ohinenutu, where two rival hostelries claimed our attention. The first is kept by a Maori, Ari Katera, or Harry Carter, and the food and lodging are said to be excellent of their kind, but his house was full of semi-intoxicated natives from Napier, whilst outside the door groups of young girls were dancing the voluptuous and disgusting "haka," so we preferred taking beds at Bennett's, where we found nothing but a semi-Anglicised hut, with execrable accommodation.

The Arawas, to whom the village belongs, are a most

consummate race of thieves, and actually boast of their descent from the greatest thief in the Island; it is unsafe to leave your horse's side at the inn door after dismounting, for if you turn your back a minute, these rogues will purloin the saddle or bridle in the twinkling of a duck's eye. Quite recently some horse-races took place here, and I was assured that very few of the visitors took their horses back with them. Nay, worse than that, some of them had been bathing, and imprudently left their clothes on the shore of the lake without anyone to watch them. When they left the water, everything down to their boots had disappeared, and they had to sit there till a messenger could be sent to borrow blankets from the inn for temporary apparel. As a rule, I found these men, who were our allies during the war (not that they liked us more, but they liked the rebels less), much inferior to the natives in the Hau-hau villages; the latter are evidently the patriots of New Zealand, and had a noble, upright bearing, that contrasted very favourably with the cringing manners of the semi-civilized scum of these lake districts. All the Arawas wear a small white feather stuck in the hair on the side of the head; and in this way our soldiers used to distinguish them during the war; when, however, they rarely lent us any active assistance, but turned out only when victory had already declared itself on our side.

Within two or three miles of the shore is the island of Mokoia, to which the fair Hinemoia is said to have swum, "suspended by a string of gourds round her neck," on a visit to her lover, Toutanikai, whose music had engaged her affections, thus reversing the story of Leander and Hero. The identical flute on which the Maori Orpheus played, like Oliver Cromwell's skull, is in the possession of at least two gentlemen, who positively assert that their own and no other is the genuine thing. The first I saw at Kaiteriria, in the possession of Cap. Mair; it is made from a human thigh bone, and is undoubtedly of great antiquity; the other, which is fully as old, but made of wood, and played from the top like a flageolet, Sir George Grey showed me in his house at the Kawau, shortly before I left the Colony.

Shortly before retiring for the night, I donned a costume suitable for the occasion, viz., a blanket, or modern toga, and boots, and stalked forth under the guidance of a small Maori boy to a sheltered bay at the end of the village, where I found a number of the inhabitants (irrespective of sex) undergoing a preparatory stew themselves, whilst they cooked their potatoes and calabash for their evening meal in a boiling hole hard by. I joined the conversazione in the water, and found that I was actually bathing on the spot where the great geyser used formerly to rise, as shown in the frontispiece of Lt Meade's Hot Lakes. I had looked in vain for this object during the afternoon; but I believe it is beyond a doubt that subterranean action is gradually subsiding near Ohinemutu, and this among other minor wonders has almost disappeared. A cold southerly wind also rendered the temperature more than usually low in this inlet. Whilst walking back to the inn, and carefully picking my way among the "ngahaus," Captain Mair told me that, when up here during the war to enlist recruits among the Arawas, he refused to pass an old man who was evidently superannuated for service. The native took his rejection so much to heart, that he went off to a short distance and deliberately sat down in the midst of a boiling mud-geyser; of course, the extreme heat soon made him yell with pain, and before they could pull him out, his flesh was entirely sodden, and he died in the most excruciating agony. It was here that I had to part with my three friends from Auckland, as they were unable to continue the journey with me to Napier, and I did so with great regret. After spending a day in a visit to the Ngae, formerly a mission station, and now the telegraph office of the district, and obtaining a glimpse of Roto-Ehu, a cold lake of great beauty, I started alone towards Lake Taupo. As I rode along the shores of Rotorua, I picked up some curious "felt balls," which were probably composed of the roots of fibrous plants, and rolled into this shape by the action of subaqueous geysers. When about three miles from Ohinemutu, I came to an unpleasantly deep creek, with hot springs on both sides; a curious feature about it being, that if the horse happened to break through the crust underneath the cold stratum, he would have found himself in a lower stratum of scalding mud. I never felt entirely easy about fording these New Zealand rivers. However minute the directions given might be, a sudden "freshet," or a new crossing, was sure to render them of doubtful benefit. The preliminary pause on the bank, the ripple of the water as it gradually rose above the saddle at the deepest point, and the sigh of relief as we emerged on the opposite side, to speculate on the next ford, are among my least agreeable reminiscences of inland travel in New Zealand. Not much further on than this, I came to a swamp of doubtful depth, which I subsequently found was really not more than up to a horse's fetlocks; but "discretion being the better part of valour," I thought I would dismount and drive the mare across in front of me. The cunning brute bolted on reaching hard ground, and I spent a weary hour and a half chasing her, over plains, up mountain gullies, in swamps, with a blazing sun overhead, till I was ready to drop with vexation and fatigue. I did not dare to let her get out of sight for a minute, or I should have been benighted on the plain, with no blankets or food. Besides this she had my saddle and bridle, bag of oats, and whole brief of necessaries on her back, which would have been a serious loss in such a forsaken part of the country as this. At last she joined some wild native horses, and began to feed, the bridle dropped over her head and became entangled with her fore feet, and I made a successful rush to secure the runaway.

After crossing a hot river, and passing a large mud-geyser, I halted by a little brook of water, clear as crystal, and made my luncheon off the water-cress, which I found growing there in abundance, and enjoyed the frugal meal very heartily. The whole of that day I did not see a human being or animal of any kind, nothing but a lifeless expanse of fern and flax; so that I felt glad at dusk to see the mighty Waikato again rolling at my feet, while on the summit of a neighbouring hill, across the river, the "pah" of Orakei-korako promised me shelter and food for the night. A loud "cooee" brought the natives down to the ferry, and I soon found myself seated in a genuine Maori accommodation house, eating bacon and potatoes with a real ivory-handled knife and fork, and drinking tea from a china tea-cup and saucer, which the hostess produced with pardonable pride, in lieu of the tin pannikin which I had already laid on the table for my own use. Before resuming the route next morning, I recrossed the river to examine "The Alum Cave," certainly not the least beautiful sight in the district, the entrance to which is most gracefully shaded by gigantic tree-ferns, and pendent stag's horn moss; the chasm apparently extends for some distance beyond the entrance chamber in which one stands, but all the passages from it are closed by a pool of very transparent tepid water, strongly impregnated with alum; the walls and dome are encrusted with salts of various kinds and colours, red, white, and green predominating; and the *tout ensemble* reminded me so strongly of the transformation scenes in the pantomimes of one's childhood, that I was disappointed to find no fairies there to welcome me to their retreat. Both banks of the river are alive with geysers, and the terraces are second only to those of Rotomahana. I was favourably impressed with the moderate charges of my Maori landlord; he charged me only "five heringi" (shillings) for my tea, bed, and breakfast, everything, though simple, being very clean.

I had little difficulty in finding my way now without a guide; for although the telegraph posts would sometimes leave me for half-a-mile, and take a short cut over some ravine or hill-top, I was always pretty sure of the direction in which I was travelling, and I found that most of the Maori tracks showed better in the twilight than during the day time, from the white sand which had washed down into them and contrasted with the surrounding darkness. On a later occasion, when I lost my way in the "bush," and had to sit down hopelessly for four hours, until the moon shone out, and the Southern Cross gave me my bearings, I could see the narrow line of road stretching away for miles across the hills, like a sparkling band of silver.

But after a dreary ride, through hills clouded in mist, and reminding me forcibly of Connemara, from the almost universal absence of trees, and scanty cultivation, I suddenly came upon a well-constructed dray-road, some distance before reaching Oruanui Pah, which I followed nearly all the way to Napier. It is a continuation of the great coach-road from Napier to Lake Taupo, an undertaking, suggested I believe by Mr. Ormond (Minister of Public Works), likely to do more for maintaining peace between Maories and settlers than any number of red-coats or breech-loading rifles. Instead of spending money as heretofore on fighting the natives, the present policy is to expend the same amount in giving employment to them on road works through their own country, in establishing secular schools in the villages, and in restoring the trade and agriculture, which (seventeen years ago) made it possible for a white man to visit safely any part of the Island. As I ascended the steep hill, from the summit of which I was to see Taupo Moana (for the Maories call this lake Moana, or sea, from its extent, though equally fresh with the waters of the other island lakes, such as Roto-Rua, Roto-Mahana, &c.), the vegetation began to change; and instead of the manuka, with its white blossoms, a blackish-looking broom covered the entire country, except where tall white columns dotted here and there announced the presence of geysers, constantly blowing off steam like a dozen locomotives at high pressure. The deep cuttings and frequent land-slips showed me that nearly the whole of the higher grounds were marine deposits of fossil shells, upheaved by a convulsion of nature which has not yet entirely subsided. In fact, as several people have said, New Zealand ought not to have been inhabited for another cycle or two, for in the South Island you have glaciers and snow torrents grinding down the mountain range, and gradually raising the level of the plains on the sea-coast with the shingle and boulders they bring down; whilst up North, vast tracts of lands are in a constant state of chemical change; and though Wellington rather monopolizes the treat of five or six annual earthquakes, nearly all the country south of the Waikato districts to beyond Taupo Lake is still actively volcanic, and resembles one great laboratory on the grandest scale.

On riding down to the ferry, at a point where the whole volume of the Waikato flows straight out of Lake Taupo in full grandeur, like the goddess Minerva from the head of her father Jove, I found a solitary native putting out from the land to fish in a very crazy canoe, and made him understand I wished to "cross" myself and horse. When we reached the other side, and I asked how much he intended to charge me, instead of giving any rational answer, he began to dance and laugh, with a kind of suppressed mum um um, which made me think he was an idiot. I tried him with "hickapenny" (sixpence) for myself, and ditto for the horse, at which he again commenced his antics with an expression of intense delight. I afterwards found he was deaf and dumb, but, nevertheless, one of the sharpest lads in the tribe.

Judge of my surprise, on riding up to the inn, to find myself suddenly in the midst of civilisation. Two days before my arrival, Cap. Bowers, a survivor of the memorable charge of the Six Hundred at Balaclava, who has been for some time connected with the commissariat of the armed constabulary hereabouts, had opened this little hostelry in time to welcome the Governor and his suite on their overland tour. Food for man and beast in abundance was there, and creature comforts to which I had long been a stranger. Fresh butter from Canterbury, oats from Napier, beef and mutton, a German baker who gave us the best and cheapest bread I had eaten since I left England, Turkish bath-towels, arm-chairs, and looking-glasses, had magically made their appearance on a spot which six months ago was "the abomination of desolation," and afforded but a scanty support to the poorest tribe in all New Zealand. The only objectional feature about the place was the canteen, where a crowd of drunken natives were squatting before the door, ready to sponge on the newest arrival for another glass of their beloved waipero (stinking water), the curse of their race here as in America. There is a lurking devilry in these people, which occasionally peeps out, as with Mahomedans; and though the men seldom indulge in private quarrels, but reserve all their savagery for war, I saw a woman suddenly display her wild nature in a way that almost made me shudder. She was a decidedly pretty girl, with an exquisite figure, set off to advantage by a black riding-habit and natty little hat; and she had been displaying her horsemanship by racing with some friends at full gallop in front of the house; when the husband came up, and, feeling irritated at her conduct in fatiguing his horse on the eve of a journey, he attempted to pull her off the saddle. She stuck to her seat like a Centaur, or rather Amazon, but her dress was torn in the struggle; as soon as he desisted, she leapt off herself, with a shriek like a madwoman, and struck him several times with her whip. He simply took her up in his arms and threw her down; satisfied with recovering his horse, which he led away. Springing to her feet again, her heaving bosom half uncovered, her long black hair streaming in the wind, her eyes glaring, and her pearl-white teeth gnashing defiance, she seized a large piece of pumicestone in her hands, and, running up behind, dashed it with her full force against his temple. I thought the man would have fallen to the ground; but he merely staggered a moment, and then, without the least retaliation, smiled disdainfully at her, and walked off to the canteen. He even took no notice when she yelled after him "Tutua," or low-born one, the most deadly insult one can offer a Maori, whose distinctions of caste are even more exclusive than those of our own upper ten. Ask a man, who is attempting to impose on you, "Who was your grandfather?" and he will generally collapse, unless he happens to be a "rangatira" of real blue blood, when you may expect a string of epithets to be hurled at you in return, as he enumerates his ancestry from the remotest ages. The little children of six years old learn this lesson before any other from their mothers' lips, and can rattle off a pedigree as long as your arm almost as soon as they talk.

I believe that any nobleman, of acknowledged long descent, would have a far better chance of buying a large block of land out here, than some rich parvenu who had made himself. The Governor and his party were away down the lake, and near the great mud-geyser of Tokano, where they were holding a "korero," or talk, with some of the chiefs; and as it is extremely hard to find one's way there by land, in consequence of the numerous swamps near the shore, and the official whale-boats which are used here were already in requisition, I resolved to spend my day profitably in visiting the great Huka (Sugar) Falls, which are said to equal, if not surpass, those of Schaffhausen on the Rhine. As I rode down the right bank of the river, I saw an extremely curious geyser called the "Crow's Nest," the incrustations of which exactly resemble sticks laid across each other in that shape. A short way further on, we came to a hot creek, in which I would have bathed with more pleasure had the temperature been less, for I came out of the water the colour of a boiled lobster. It is becoming a famous resort for invalids from Napier, who next year will be able to travel all the way by coach (two days' journey); and besides its efficacy in curing rheumatism, scrofulous affections, &c., they have the additional advantage of Captain Bower's comfortable house on the lake close by at Tapuehararu (Sounding Footsteps), thus named because, when riding,

"Quadrupedante putrem sonitu quatit angula campum,"

in the most audible manner, and one not reassuring to a nervous person, who cannot help but speculate on the thickness of the crust on the earth's surface in this spot, however disinclined to scientific research in general.

About two miles down the river, I recrossed the hot creek where it joins the Waikato, and tethered my horse in a little meadow of the coarse native grass and young flax-plant. On entering the settlement, I found two old women peeling potatoes, who reluctantly consented to take me over the river. The canoe in which we embarked was of the crankiest kind. I was afraid to sneeze or cough for fear of an upset, and kept my eyes steadily fixed on the centre of the boat, with a hand on each side to balance it. There was some difficulty in picking one's way for a mile, through the tall raupo (rush) and tohi-grass; but I soon heard the distant roar of the falls, and caught sight of the rapids at the head, where the stream suddenly narrows to about fifty yards. In the centre were some black rocks, with piebald shags perched on them, watching intently for the fish as they darted beneath them; whilst immediately below this the water leaped up in convulsed masses of green, pink, and white froth, like the great whirlpool below Niagara Suspension Bridge. I crept cautiously over the huge boulders along the bank, in which sundry suspicious cracks indicated an impending addition to the debris of rock, and came shortly upon a scene of the utmost grandeur. The whole force of the river breaks over the edge in a fan of feathery sugar-like spray into the basin beneath. This is fringed on all sides with a wonderful variety of evergreen over-hanging shrubs, any one of which would be prized in an English garden. Whilst peeping over the precipice, one can see where the green eddies of water have undermined the rock far beyond the ledge on which one stands. The hill sides are clothed with a dense scrub of the tutu, a treacherous bush with dark bright-green leaves, which have the effect of either killing outright the cattle which imprudently eat it, or intoxicating them to such an extent that the eyes become glazed, and the brain giddy, and for a day or more they are unable to walk.

My great regret in visiting all these new scenes was,

that I did so generally alone, which destroys half one's pleasure. One ought to have a travelling companion, both for the sake of a little human sympathy and society, when crossing these lonely tracts, and also in case of any accident which, as we all know, will occur in the best regulated equipages. There is, too, a great delight in talking over past experiences in after life at a comfortable fireside, or with your feet under the mahogany; but the deaf adders, who have not seen the spots which you may be describing, and who have not shared the adventures of your route, refuse (reasonably enough) to open their ears, charm you never so wisely. In fact, they think you are talking "shop," as we used to say at College; *i.e.*, monopolising the conversation on a subject which is familiar and intensely interesting to yourself alone of all the company present. I have been asked whether my lonely rides never suggested thoughts which would never have occurred to me "in the busy hum of cities and of men;" but, to me, nature never wears her brightest guise unless I have some one to share her delights with me. Men do, it is true, get to love a solitary life, and, like the prisoner who had been all his life confined in the Bastille, cannot bear to face the world again; but this is a morbid, unhealthy frame of mind, which should be sedulously discouraged, for

"He liveth best who loveth best;"

and what is the love of a recluse but selfishness.

On my return from the waterfall, I stopped at the mouth of the hot creek, and had a sensation bathe. The modus operandi was to climb up a little waterfall, shoot down the smooth rock channel about six feet into the pool beneath, then recline for an interval in the comfortable stone arm-chair formed there by nature, enjoying a douche or shower-bath; and, finally, to brace one's relaxed energies by a dive into the invigorating waters of the Waikato, which passed the mouth of the little brook, with only a bar of sand between the cold and warm currents.

When Sir George Bowen and his cavalcade arrived in the evening, I introduced myself to him as a fellow-Oxonian, and he immediately (much to my relief) asked me to make use of the house, the whole of which had been exclusively engaged for him during his stay. Of course, I gladly accepted the offer, in preference to continuing my journey, especially as the next day there was to be a "korero," or talk with the Ngatimaniapoto, which was quite a novelty to me.

Immediately after breakfast, Poihepe, one of the seven chiefs who signed the treaty of Waitangi ceding the sovereignty of the Islands to Queen Victoria, came to conduct the Governor to the verandah of a neighbouring house, where we found the whole village assembled in front of us. The meeting was addressed first by Poihepe; and, although I am told he is a great diplomat, and a really able man, his speech appeared to me to consist of—"Haere mai, come hither, O Governor"—then a grunt of self-approval, and a little walk up and down the arena; "haere mai, haere mai, for the Pakeka and Maori are at peace"—grunt, walk, nod of approval, etc., etc. None of the speakers ever seemed nervous; they uttered their sentences very deliberately, and the rule was, when at a loss, say "haere mai." It seemed to be the custom in their runanga, or meeting, for young men to be put on their legs for practice; whilst all, even women, are listened to with equal gravity and attention. Some of those present had been leading rebels during the war; *e. g.*, Hoani Makau, from Orakei-Korako; but all alike expressed the same wish for schools, roads, and commerce, that Poihepe did. This chief, though in the heart of the disaffected country, was our steadfast ally throughout the recent war, and had led his small body of men against Te Kooti, the instigator of the Poverty Bay massacre, when the latter was still the popular favourite with a large number of followers. Arete (Alice), his wife, was the most matronly and handsome woman I met. She must have been also an unusually skilled housekeeper; for I heard rumours of fat pigeons and ducks, which she bones in the most skilful way, and puts up in casks for her lord's use. One fault she has—she's a little too fond of her grog; but then, Poihepe himself is a man who thinks nothing of his two bottles of brandy after dinner. The korero might have been indefinitely prolonged, for, like all colonials, they are much given to "yarning," and generally keep it up till some peculiarly happy metaphor, in which they largely deal, takes the fancy of the majority, and the debate terminates in applause and acclamation.

I was most interested in one of their "waiata," or songs of welcome, which they introduce as we might do quotations from Homer or Shakespeare, and which went down with the audience to any extent. Mary, the pretty girl whom I had seen in such a state of ungovernable fury the previous afternoon, was sitting in the midst of her friends; and as she smiled coquettishly while they performed a new edition of the haka, kneeling (for every village has its own peculiar style of dance), I could scarcely believe her to be the same woman. I was once surprised in the very same way by some Arabs at Tripoli. They had been educated at the French school in Algiers, and were the quietest, most European-like girls, to all appearance. But one evening, when, by special request, I had allowed their husbands to invite the hadra, or religious club, to the house, and the tomtoms had struck up their dizzy, monotonous thrill, I suddenly found that the women's faces had all disappeared from the gallery above; and on going upstairs, I discovered them with their hair tossed, and eyes rolling like demons, in the full frenzy of the dance. I stopped them, with some difficulty, for none of them were able to recognise me; their teeth were fast clenched, as if in a fit, and they moaned piteously; and the spectators urged me to let them dance the devil out. But how sickened and disgusted I felt at the sight! All the polish was on the surface:

> "Naturam expellas furcâ tamen usque recurrit,
> Et mala (?) perrumpt fastidia."

You cannot tame a Maori or an Arab thoroughly, and it is a fact that many of the half-castes in New Zealand have a strong tendency to resume their savage nature and rejoin their tribes, after becoming apparently so civilised as to thoroughly adopt the habits of Europeans.

Luckily, before I left Taupo, I made the acquaintance of Major L., who gave me letters ensuring a warm reception at all the Constabulary posts on the road to Napier. I may here say that this body of cavalry is virtually the standing army of the colony. It numbers about eight hundred; both officers and privates are a splendid lot of fellows, very intelligent, and with a strong *esprit de corps*. They may well be proud of the force to which they belong, for most of them distinguished themselves by acts of gallantry during the war, which are but ill rewarded by the universal New Zealand medal, and a most scanty pay. Sir Charles Dilke's story of admitting none but elder sons of British peers, old army officers, and members of the two great English universities to the force, contains, like most jests, an undercurrent of truth, for you really do meet here and among the gum-diggers in the north, the strangest mixture of refinement and rough life.

At my first halting place, Opepe, a little block-fort on

the edge of a lovely bush, I met an old French priest, Father Rény, who told me that he had been out here as a missionary for thirty years. He impressed upon me the fact that the cloudless days of mid-winter lend additional enchantment to the shores of Taupo, for then a perfect view is obtained of the grand volcano of Tongariro, and the still more lofty peak of Ruapeho in the distance, clad in a spotless robe of eternal snow. The legend of the mountains is, that Ruapeho and Mount Egmont were both giants who fell desperately in love with the snowy bosom and sparkling eyes of the lady-mountain, Tongariro; but Ruapeho being the stronger kicked his adversary right across to the East Coast at Taranaki, where he still sulks in solitary grandeur; not that he should do so, for what Mount Domett is to Dunedin, or Mount Wellington to Hobarton, that Mount Egmont now is to Taranaki, the pride and pet of all the patriotic beauties of New Plymouth, a fact which ought fully to compensate him for his rejection by Tongariro.

At Runanga, a very exposed block-house on a bare hill-top, I spent my next evening, gaining shelter in time to escape a drenching storm which beat down from one of the three great mountain ranges between Taupo and Napier.

After showing me "the Institute," where, to my surprise, I found all the English illustrated papers, and most of the home magazines and reviews, which are thus passed on from post to post for the men's recreation, and telling me how an old friend in the "force" had edited a comic manuscript fortnightly with great success whilst stationed here, my host, Captain G——, entertained me, as we sat before a comfortable wood fire, with an inexhaustible repertoire of Maorilore and legend.

"Their very name," said he, "of 'Maori,' or 'pure,' is

a misnomer. It may be, and probably is true that the Hawaians or Samoans immigrated here in olden times; but in all probability they murdered the weaker race of Morioris, whom they found indigenous to the islands, and then, as took place in the Chatham group quite recently, the women became the wives of their conquerors, and, as is invariably the case, introduced many words into the language, by the education of their children, which are entirely distinct from either the Malay or Hawaian dialects. This theory would explain the variety of tints observable in different families, even those belonging to one tribe.

"The Maori is a strangely excitable creature, so much so that from purely working on his imagination he will turn sick suddenly and lay down to die, with no apparent ailment beyond the fright caused by the witchcraft of his enemy. There are two tribes in particular, one of which is the Uriwera, who are able to makutu, or bewitch people in this way, and I heard some stories illustrative of the terror with which the power is regarded among them.

"In the first case, an old chief was reputed to have made several of his grandchildren waste away by his enchantments. His son and daughter-in-law were, of course, inconsolable for their loss, and carefully kept their surviving child, a little boy, out of reach. One fine day, however, they discovered that the lad was sitting by the side of the old man, who was hoeing potatoes in the field. The father took down his tomahawk, and creeping up cautiously, lest he himself should be makutu-ed by a look, brained his parent on the spot to save the child's life. He was considered by his neighbours to have performed a most heroic and noble act, as at the sacrifice of his own filial affection he had rid them of a wizard universally dreaded and hated."

Captain G——'s other anecdote was even more startling

than the above. Tamaika, an Uriwera chief, had been down to Opotiki, on the east coast, and, when passing through a village on his return to the interior, asked a favour of some native girl which she refused him. Pointing to her with his finger, he said, "I makutu you." This took place on a Saturday afternoon, and early on Monday morning, the girl, who had at once taken to her bed, died without any apparent symptoms of disease or poison. My informant on this occasion told me that he had been to visit the patient, and attempted to argue her out of the superstition which was killing her. "Yes," she said, "it may seem foolish, but then you can't feel as I do. White men can't be bewitched as we are, and my death is certain."

This strong belief in supernatural power sometimes leads to good effects. I saw a half-caste lad at Tauranga who some time ago had been warned by the doctor that he could not survive three months; and he was, in fact, in the last stage of consumption. His native relations, however, came and begged leave to exercise their power of makutu on him. He was so weak at that time that they actually had to carry him to their canoe, in which they conveyed him to an island not far from Tauranga, where he remained under their treatment for a few weeks, and when I saw him, he was strong enough to undergo a long day's journey on horseback. I asked what they had given him in the way of medicine, and he said, "Nothing at all; they fed me on fish and potatoes, and no one was allowed to touch my head for a week or two, and here I am again, half restored to health!"

Travellers often hear stories about the unchastity of the Maori women. Although this may be the case among the unmarried girls, who base their claim to be considered " belle of the village " on the number of intrigues they can boast of, one rarely finds instances of infidelity after marriage ; the penalty is too serious—for the woman, probably death,—for the man, "utu" or confiscation of his available property.

Next morning, to my dismay, no horse could be found ; my mare had broken down a rail of the "government paddock," and wandered off into the woods in company with a "wild horse," which had been hanging about the enclosure of late. The men went out to look for her, and succeeded in capturing her companion too. He was a queer object ; he had evidently been living in the forest for years ; and from want of rapid exercise in open ground, (for the supple-jacks, a kind of climbing black cane, impede a beast's progress very much in the bush, and frequently strangle it in its terrified efforts to escape), his hoofs had grown to an enormous length, so that he almost resembled some new species of quadruped.

The next twelve miles of the road to Tarawera are as yet quite incomplete, and it is marvellous to see how the poor pack-horses have worn regular steps or ladders up the sides of nearly perpendicular hills, by which they climb to the top with the agility of cats. Every now and then I met long trains carrying up oats and stores of all kinds to the interior, led by a sober old beast with a bell round his neck, the sound of which they follow like sheep.

To compensate, however, for the hardships of the road, it lies through the most glorious bush I have seen in the island, with cascades and rivers as beautiful as those in the western highlands of Scotland. Besides gigantic tree-ferns, rata with its scarlet blossoms, and kahikatea pine in clean spars of two hundred feet in height, one is fascinated by the variety of creepers and ferns near the running water, more especially the dense undergrowth of the Prince of Wales' Feather (*Leptopteris Superba*), whose dark green mossy fronds lose their velvet-like softness very rapidly on exposure to the sun. I tried very hard to send home specimens of this rare fern, which is even more luxuriant here than near Hokitika in the South, and also some plants of variegated flax (*Phormium Colensoii variegata*); but they began to turn a suspicious brown on landing in San Francisco, and I bequeathed them to Woodward's Gardens on the chance of obtaining duplicates if I ever visit the States again. At Tarawera, there is a snug little inn for visitors, and a hot spring, to which one ought to be acclimatised, for I came out of the rough wooden tub on the hill-side as red as a lobster, and with a disagreeable tightness about the forehead. In fact it is very imprudent to indulge oneself in these baths at random, or too often, without medical advice. They bring on a kind of "crisis" after a week or two, when the body is subject to painful boils, which however are said to disappear with all other ailments by persevering in the waters. It may have been poor diet in the Maori country that brought me down in physique, but I was completely laid up for a time at Napier in this way.

The country hereabouts is very curiously constituted; the ground seems firm enough to cut, but as soon as the top binding of fern is removed, there are perpetual landslips of the soft pumice and gravel underneath, which involve constant care; also, as far as I could see, all the pasture is on the very tops of the high-mountain plateaus, and in the valleys there is nothing but raupo or flax.

On Titiowharu, where I slept the next night, I found the overseer (to whom Mr. C——, at Hamilton, had franked me,) "mustering" sheep, which is the next important process to "shearing" in the squatter's annual programme. The rams and ewes are divided and subdivided; whilst the poor little lambs, before they go out of the fold again, "leave their tails behind them," as little Bopeep would say, and also have their ears punched and backs marked with raddle or tar. It is customary to invite all the neighbours to your "muster," as they can then pick out their missing sheep which have strayed from the adjoining runs. As they complete each flock, it is turned over to a shepherd, who would drive it off with the aid of his dogs to a beat, possibly ten or twenty miles distant, for these squatters own enormous tracts of land about here.

To show you some of the peculiarities of New Zealand travel, I may mention that between this and Napier, I crossed one little river forty-two times in about ten miles, though it is only fair to say that none of the fords were at all deep or dangerous. There were numbers of natives on the road from town, well mounted, and dressed up to the eyes in the latest fashions; for in Hawke's Bay some of them are extremely wealthy, and you may see Maories in black frock-coats and tall hats, sitting in their carriage and pair there; men, too, who consider themselves judges of brandy, and talk of their "Hennessy" as we might do of Sandeman's port, or Roëderer's carte-blanche champagne. One old gentleman was most indignant lately at being offered "Beehive" brand instead of his favourite mark, and threatened to withdraw his custom from the unfortunate spirit merchant who had dared to suggest such a change.

Napier is a small but rather pretty town, built on a high spit of land facing the sea; the harbour runs in behind the town to the north, and is not accessible to large steamers.

Here, as elsewhere in New Zealand, one meets now and then with social anomalies which one can look at sometimes from a ludicrous, as well as a distressing point of view. For instance, when I was looking about, on my arrival at the hotel, for some stables in which to put up my horse, I suddenly felt a tap on the shoulder, and heard a "How d' ye do?" from a nice looking young fellow whose face I had some difficulty at first in recalling. It was N——, a pupil of the same tutor as myself at Eton; and here he had taken to keeping a livery stable in Napier and driving a hansom in the streets for hire. Most of the residents knew his history, and looked upon the whole affair rather as a joke than otherwise; so much so that they did not hesitate to offer him their hospitality, and ladies would always bow on meeting him, unless he was actually on the box driving. They told me an amusing story of his experience. Col. Russell, the Minister of Instruction, hired the hansom for a ball in the neighbourhood; and on reaching the door of the house, gave N—— directions to return for him at one a.m.; N—— touched his hat and drove off, but had not gone far down the carriage-road before he stopped, took the horse out and tethered him to a tree, and slipping off his mackintosh, came back to the house in full evening dress, having received an invitation also himself. The evening wore out, and morning arrived. About three o'clock, someone walked up to Col. Russell, whom he saw leaning against the wall, and looking rather annoyed, and remarked to him, "Why, Russell, I thought you were an early bird; what are you doing at the ball still?" "Well," said the Colonel, "I had intended to go home about two hours ago, but there's that confounded cabby of mine engaged for three more dances, and I can't get away till he's done."

After a short visit to Rissington, the proprietor of which, Colonel W., told me he could ride forty miles in a straight line on his own "sheep run," I took passage in the "*Rangatira,*" a very diminutive steamer chiefly employed in the cattle-trade, for Tauranga, a fine harbour on the east coast, south of Cape Colville. We stopped twice on the voyage to take in wool, once at Poverty Bay, the scene of Te Kooti's great massacre, and afterwards at Tolago Bay, where we saw the little cove in which Captain Cook hauled up his vessel for repairs. Here a solitary white man came off, steering a large whale-boat manned by natives in very primitive and scanty costume. I could not help congratulating myself that I was not stranded like him in this lonely spot, without newspapers or letters for months together. I heard a good deal of Te Kooti's exploits as I rode across the island, which I must record here. Since the war there have been three malcontents among the rebels, who steadily refused to accept terms, and were a constant source of terror to the settlers, viz., Kereopa, Tito Kiwaru, and Te Kooti. Kereopa was the man who murdered Volkner, the missionary, and ate his eyes; he was hung in Napier, shortly before I arrived there. Tito Kiwaru received a free pardon on condition of abandoning his evil ways, and settled down quietly near Taranaki; but Te Kooti, the great Hau-hau leader, has for the last three years baffled all the energy and perseverance of his pursuers, though his band of three hundred followers has gradually dwindled down to something less than half-a-dozen, including women. After his escape from the Chatham Islands, he wandered about in the bush, occasionally pouncing down upon some unprotected farmhouse, and burning it, but beyond this leaving no visible sign of his whereabouts. Almost constantly there were three or four bodies of constabulary on his track; but partly owing to the secret support he received from those natives who dared not openly sympathise with him, and partly from the fact that even the hardiest white men cannot subsist on berries and fern-roots for any length of time, (and it was impossible to carry many stores through such a maze of hills and forests,) Te Kooti, though living a miserable hand-to-mouth existence, and hunted down from camp to camp frequently only a few hours in advance of his enemies, was still enabled to elude them. When asked the nature of the country hereabouts, a native will hold up his hand and show you the spaces between his fingers; it is an endless succession of ridges and valleys, so that it is impossible to get an extended view. "It is like looking for a needle in a haystack," said one of the officers, "and we shall never catch him unless they employ bloodhounds or Australian blacks to track him." Once a party actually caught sight of him scaling a cliff in front of them, and attempted to discharge their guns, but the caps and powder had become so damp by constant exposure to the damp weather, that they would not ignite. At last, after he was finally supposed to be hemmed in somewhere on the east coast, and a sensational paragraph had appeared at least once a week in the Auckland papers, announcing "the imminent capture of Te Kooti," we suddenly heard of his appearance in the Waikato, right on the other side of the island, whence he made his escape into the "king's country" and claimed protection from Tawhiao, who seems inclined to let him live there, on the condition that he causes no further disturbances. Leaving aside the consideration of his guilt, it seems almost better to withdraw the price set on his head, and not to risk the chance of another fight by insisting on his extradition. He has lost his influence, and we should only make a martyr of him by any further action on our part, so that " quieta non movere " seems to be the best policy.

I had made up my mind to leave the steamer at Tauranga, and try to ride overland to Ohinemuri, where I could get a boat down to the Thames gold-fields; but, as the *Rangatira* steamed off from the wharf and left me standing there in a drenching rain, my heart rather sank as I remembered the warnings my friends had given me about travelling after the summer had broken and the wet season set in. However, the best face had to be put on the matter now, so I went off to the inn, and there stopped for two whole days, reading Gulliver's Travels and looking from the window at the steady down-pour from a dull leaden sky which never seemed likely to clear. On the third morning however, seeing enough blue heavens to make a Dutchman's breeches, I imprudently chartered a boat to begin my journey, against the advice of my landlord who told me the creeks would be "up" still, and I should be unable to cross them. Off we started on our weary useless journey down the harbour, and crossed the little forest of mangroves which divide the Tauranga and Kati-kati tides, just as the bush tops began to peep out of the rapidly receding waters. At the little hostelry, kept by a half-caste, Alf. Faulkner, I found him and his two brothers ruefully regarding the sunset, which certainly had a suspiciously liquid appearance; they were intending to start next day for the races at Ohinemuri, and told me that I might try the experiment with them. As they were about the best guides in the district, and thoroughly up in bush travel, I thought myself almost at my journey's end; but, like the young bear, all my troubles were before me. That night and all next day we had a terrific thunderstorm, and the ceaseless patter of the heavy drops on the corrugated iron roof, told us that the difficulties of the road were hourly increasing, and that I should have much delay and vexation of spirit before I got to Auckland again. However, I could not complain of my quarters, the beds were clean, and Polly, our pretty Maori hostess (the neatest and most good-natured of girls possible, and far superior to any native woman I have met before or since) gave us the best plum-pudding I have tasted since leaving

England, and introduced me also to a delicious preserve made of "pie melon" cut into little squares, and very much like Everton toffee in flavour.

At last (our patience being exhausted) my cicerone, Alf. Faulkner, thought we would try to force our way across the country; "we could but turn back again, and it would be such a pity to miss the first race-meeting of the Thames natives." His wife prudently slipped a bottle of gin and some slices of cold plum-pudding into her husband's wallet before starting, which, as experience proved, was a a very needful precaution.

The Maories generally commence a journey as fast as their horses will carry them; and I am afraid in this case we were no exception to the rule. We galloped the first five miles along a hard sandy beach, with the waves occasionally dashing up to our horses' fetlocks, and then began a slow and tedious ascent by the Kati-kati pass to a plain of about twenty miles in width, which, people say, is to be before very long the great alluvial gold-field of this island. It has not been "prospected" yet, from the reluctance of the natives to mining encroachments; but some residents in Tauranga, who possess influence with them, and who think their own little town is destined to become the "hub of the Antipodes," eclipsing even Grahamstown or Hokitika in the rapidity of its growth, are already taking steps to secure concessions from some of the leading chiefs, under which they will develop the resources of the "field" for the benefit of the native landlords. And here our misfortunes began; the first creek we came to should have convinced us that we need go no further, for what was usually a little brooklet had swollen into a large torrent, which rose nearly to the saddle-girths of our horses, as they cautiously picked their steps across the treacherous-looking ford. Each creek in succession grew worse and worse; at some there were falls and rapids not a hundred yards below where we crossed, which threatened an untimely end in the event of one false step on the slippery black rocks, over which the water was now rushing with unusual force; at others the steep banks had become so greasy, that when our horses had slid rather than walked down the zigzag path to the water, they became hopelessly bogged in the stream, till we hauled the poor brutes by main force up the opposite bank. At last we came to a ford, over which our leader decided we should have to swim them, at the cost of getting thoroughly wet through. Accordingly, in we plunged, and down they went, with their heads just rising above the surface of the water. It is a most unpleasant feeling to have the ripple gradually creeping higher and higher, until it reaches the waist. Unfortunately, like most young travellers, I had neglected to guard against such a contingency. I suddenly remembered that my watch, matches and tobacco were getting soaked, instead of being safely stowed in my hat, as they should have been;. but "sweet are the uses of adversity," and I shall know better next time. When we had ridden some twenty-five miles, and were entering a thick bush, I began to look for signs of Ohinemuri village, and almost to think my journey at an end; but to my intense disgust Alf. Faulkner informed me that *we were just coming* to "the river" (the others having been mere creeks or brooklets). After a weary walk of two miles, through mud knee deep, pausing frequently to free our horses from the overhanging supple-jacks, a species of black cane, which often entangles and throttles cattle in their terrified efforts to extricate themselves, we came to our *bête noir*, the Ohinemuri river, and as we looked down at it, "spes omnis tenues evasit in auras." It would be hopeless to attempt the ford that night; the first step would have taken us into a deep boiling eddy, a few yards below which we could hear the heavy plunge of the water as it rushed past the little island in the centre of the rapids, bending down the bushes with its impetuous force, and fell over the rocks from a considerable height into a large basin at the foot. No one in his senses would have ventured across the head of that miniature Niagara; therefore,

"Rusticus expectans inhiat dum defluat amnis."

we resolved to wait for the chances of the morrow, and before the night fell, collected the driest firewood we could find and hunted about in the bush for some branches of the karaka, the dark-green leaves of which resemble in appearance those of the camelia and would serve as provender for our famished steeds; for there was not a blade of grass in the place. From a wet canvas knapsack our own rations were served out; to every man a slice of bread and butter, a lump of plum-pudding in a semi-diluted state, and a modicum of gin which warmed our shivering frames. I was very thankful to get even this much, for we had eaten nothing since breakfast and felt a pretty good "twist" for food. This was the first occasion on which I had bivouacked in the open air; it was unusually trying, for I was the only one of the party without a dry change of clothes, and it certainly was a miserable night's experience. I spread my mackintosh on the muddy ground close to the fire, with a log of wood for my pillow, and literally steamed till morning, like a bundle of clothes from the wash. You may imagine that I hardly got a wink of sleep, for the fuel was damp, and required to be constantly replenished with small sticks and fanned to make it burn at all. Now in England the effect of all this would probably have been rheumatic fever, or inflammation of the lungs, but I can conscientiously assert that no harm at all came of it in my case. The sky, fortunately was clear; the Southern Cross shone out brightly overhead, and although there was just the slightest suspicion of frost in the air, you felt that it was an exhilarating cold full of life, and not the dismal rawness of our climate at home.

As morning approached, the clouds began to gather overhead, and drops of rain pattered down, which soon roused us from our uncomfortable couches. I went down to the river bank, but, *me miserum!* instead of falling, the water had actually risen three inches since the previous evening, for I had placed a little flood-mark at the edge of the stream by which to ascertain this.

We saddled our horses, and with a settled gloom upon our faces turned back to Kati-kati. Fancy our being within three miles of our destination, within half an hour's ride of Ohinemuri and the races, and we actually had to return over the old ground (28 miles) to the place we had started from.

Such are the inglorious uncertainties of New Zealand travel! I shall know better than travel overland in the wet season when I go there next.

What aggravated my sense of failure was, that I had particularly wished to visit the grave of Taraia, a celebrated old cannibal chief, and a pensioner of our Government, who had just shuffled off this mortal coil, and been buried at Ohinemuri. There was to be a "tangi," or wake, in his honour, at which all the leading men of the North would be present, and I should have seen a really memorable feast; for on such occasions, the friends and relatives of the deceased send enormous quantities of dried eels, potatoes, rum, tea, sugar, biscuits, and, lastly, the great national delicacy of decomposed sharks' fins, on which the guests are entertained as long as the provisions last, when the ceremony of mourning also ceases. The "tangi" itself is a "keen" or low monotonous wail, which is kept up night and day over the body by the women, till the food and their endurance simultaneously give out. This process is not limited to funerals; for a Maori woman welcomes her friends by a "tangi" or whimper, and by screwing out some crocodilish tears to express, I suppose, her intense grief at their previous separation. The process is as follows:— Look as unhappy as possible, squash your nose against that of the new arrival, and make a low melancholy whine, with your lips compressed; continue the above as long as suits your taste. I have seen very affectionate old ladies sit with their noses together, and their eyes dribbling for half-an-hour together, while they crooned like two love-stricken cats. But curiously enough, they "speed the parting guest" in a far more cheerful way; then every face is wreathed in smiles; you mount your horse, and ride off amid a chorus of Haere, haere, haere (Go, go!), as long as you are within hearing-distance. This I could understand as a kind of a "God speed;" but I am afraid I once scandalised a very punctilious old dowager, who had begun to "tangi," as I came up to a pah at the Hot Lakes, by bursting into a hearty laugh at her dolorous expression of countenance. I have often since wondered whether she thought me wanting in respect; but I fancy she would possibly excuse the *faux pas* on the score of ignorance.

But to return to my story: "Misfortunes never came single;" for after we had embarked at Kati-kati on the little cutter belonging to my guide, the wind and rain suddenly stopped, and we drifted slowly the whole day on the tide towards Tauranga in a dead calm and blue sky. As I laboured away with one of the long "sweeps," punting the boat over the mangrove shallows, I almost wavered in my purpose, and thought of turning back again; but the heavy white clouds which still hung over the Cormandel ranges in the distance warned me not to trust the spiteful caprices of the weather again, and rather to make *certain* of getting home by sea, even if I had to wait a fortnight for it. We made a frugal meal about noon of bread and "pipis," a small shell-fish not unlike our mussels. Kati-kati harbour is the great fishing-ground of the Northern natives; and even when the canoes are not out, the flocks of gulls and cormorants, and other sea-fowl, make it very lively for the innumerable shoals of mullet and snapper. A child may walk into the banks at low water, and, in five or ten minutes, gather a basket of pipi, which will provide a day's food for the family. The peculiarity of these shells is their sharp knife-like edge, which makes them useful for two purposes, viz., the carving of pipes and other ornamental wood-work, at a time when Sheffield cutlery had not reached these remote regions; and secondly the important process of tattooing, an art however which is rapidly dying out before the progress of civilization. Now-a-days the women confine themselves to two blue lines along the lips, just about kissing-point, which, in my opinion, does not improve their personal appearance; whilst the men, whose heads used to form an important article of export in olden days and served as curiosities in the museums of Europe, have now become so effeminate as scarcely to undergo the tortures of tattoo in the interests of fashion. Everyone knows how the British tar loves to adorn himself with anchors and mermaids on the arm, by the simple process of pricking the flesh with a needle and rubbing in gunpowder; but the tattoo is a far more serious undertaking. The patient is placed in a reclining position, whilst the artiste deliberately nips out little particles of flesh, with his pincers of pipi-shell. The blood streams from the face, and the pain, accompanied with swelling of the parts operated upon, must be very excruciating for a time; but as the design is often really very ornamental, and serves either to inspire terror into the foe or else to distinguish families of aristocratic rank by a kind of armorial bearings, you may still occasionally see young men of Conservative proclivities keeping up the old custom with stoical endurance and hardly wincing at each fresh touch of the operator.

Well! to conclude; I had to wait at Tauranga for nearly a week before any means of escape turned up; and bereft as I was of books or friends, it was the veriest prison-house you can imagine. At last the schooner "Dauntless" arrived, and I took my passage by her to Auckland, where I arrived exactly a fortnight later than I need have done if I had kept to the slow but sure means of sea-voyage, instead of attempting overland travel *ad nauseam*. Even when we had started, the same fatality seemed to dog my footsteps, and for a whole afternoon we beat about Kati-kati with a head wind; but when I awoke early next morning, we had made half the distance, and anchored off Mercury Island to pick up a "squatter" who lived there. He came off shortly with a regular boat-load of wild-turkeys, which thrive amazingly here, and which he was taking to market in Auckland. Before noon we had rounded Cape Colville, and, much to my relief, we anchored that same evening at the Queen Street Wharf, exactly six weeks after I had started on my eventful and solitary trip across the North Island.

OUR FLAX-MILL.

The roughest month's experience I have had in New Zealand, was up in the bush, about a hundred miles north of Auckland, where my brother has been building a mill to manufacture fibre from the Phormium Tenax, a kind of gigantic aloe, which grows wild over immense areas of the land in those parts. We manage the journey as follows:—a little steamer, the "Gemini," carries us up the Waitemata River to Riverhead, about two hours' distance from Auckland; there we get the coach; or in winter, when the roads are nearly impassable, we ride on horseback for fourteen miles across the portage, to Helensville on the Kaipara Harbour; there is a railway already begun from here to Riverhead, but although the earthwork and bridges are complete, we shall have to wait for rails from England before it is opened to the public. At Helensville we find either the Government cutter, or the regular weekly mail-boat "Pai-Mariri," which takes about a day to sail eighty miles up to Mangawhare, a trading station on the Wairoa River, the future Mersey of the country and navigable for vessels of 1,000 tons for fully forty miles above this point. Here we used formerly to get into a little gig, and row for nine miles up our particular creek, the prettiest little stream imaginable, called the Kaihu; but now we have got a diminutive steam-launch, which I have christened the "Elsie," and which flies the dear old University College flag at her stern, Oxford blue with a golden cross in the centre. She can

run about eight knots an hour, and startles the flocks of wild duck which abound up our creek, as she glides swiftly along under the graceful fern-trees and giant puriri with their soft magenta flowers.

In summer, we are never at a loss for fresh meat, for you may count by dozens the large native pigeons, as they sun their bronze and purple plumage, lazily perched on the top of the totara pines, or gather in flocks to eat the berries of the puriri and karaka. They are the most stupid birds in existence, and never seem to be much frightened at the discharge of a gun, so long as they cannot see who fired it. If one only had a few English comforts and friends up here, I think it would be the pleasantest spot in existence. I have seen no bush or river scenery to equal it for quiet loveliness; there is such an immense variety of foliage on the banks, and at a very short distance from the mouth of the creek the water runs as clear as crystal between high, dense bushes of the flax (our peculiar industry), from whose pendant crimson petals, on flower-stalks nearly thirty feet high, the wild bees gather the sweetest of honey. Far away on the sky-line to the north-west, there is a mountain range extending from Monganui Bluff to Tutamoi, a high table-land with an abrupt precipitous face. You can hear the heavy boom of the breakers on the sea-coast, six miles away, where the whole force of the Western Pacific breaks upon the hard beach of white sand, along which you can gallop for hours as straight as an arrow. The cliffs here and there show great seams of lignite on their face, which makes me think that some day we shall be finding coal-fields in the neighbourhood. Indeed we are right in the line of such a discovery, for the Bay of Islands mine is but a short distance from us on the other coast.

In Mocatua, one of the creeks running down to the sea,

I found the remains of a French frigate which was wrecked there in early times. Nothing now is left but a few heavy spars and such iron rings as the Maories could not carry away. They say that Parore, one of our landlords, secured about sixty tons of gunpowder from the wreck, and has it stowed away safely in some remote corner.

But I must get back to our mill, and give a succinct historical account of it alone, for if I wander off into details of other things the world itself would not contain them all. Before my arrival, T—— had gone up with a couple of men to select a site, and clear the river of snags. They began with a series of mishaps. The first morning when they woke, they found the blankets covered with large white patches, which at first sight they thought were the drippings from their candle, but on closer examination and touch they discovered, to their intense disgust, that the whole surface was a crawling mass of maggots, which the noisy blow-flies had deposited there during the night. I think this was the worst misery of all our bush life. Fleas, Maori bugs, sand-flies and mosquitoes were bad enough in their way (and we had plenty of them), but to hear, just as you were dropping off to sleep, the loud buzz of these other loathsome insects, as they bobbed against the canvas of the tent, and then dropped on to one's blanket or clothes with malicious intent, destroyed all the romance of camping out at once. I found a way of balking them at last, by peppering, salting, and smoking everything woollen in my possession, whilst, as an additional safeguard to the meat, we always kept it covered; or, if carving at table, one of us would mount guard with a roll of newspaper to knock over our enemies, whilst the other cut off what he wanted as rapidly as possible. These plagues disappeared when we got a regular house built, for the little English fly came in swarms, and actually worried their big brothers to death. They themselves proved troublesome enough in turn, but were a vast improvement on their predecessors.

Misfortune the second was as follows: S——, one of the hands, rowed down to the store at the mouth of the creek to buy provisions, and bring back some houseblocks. We suppose the "dingy" must have caught on a snag, and, in leaning over to free it, he fell out of the boat and was drowned; for the body was found three days afterwards among some rushes in the river, whilst the "dingy" had not capsized, but was floating right side up and half full of water. His poor dog "Jonah" whined pitifully when he saw his master's dead body, and for a long time seemed quite disconsolate, but has since attached himself to us, and will not follow anyone else. When we got the stream cleared of snags, and the timber for the mill was ready, more "hands" came up, and we were rather puzzled for a time how to lodge them all as there was only one tent; but in a very short space of time they built themselves "whares," or huts, of a very ingenious kind and perfectly waterproof. The stakes at the four corners and sides were of manuka or ti-tree, while the roof and intermediate spaces were made of the spreading leaves of the "nekau" palm, which answered the purpose fully as well as the corrugated iron used by more ambitious architects. Certainly in dry weather I have seen a house like this burnt down in about a quarter of an hour; but then it really cost nothing but the half-day's labour to build another exactly similar, so that, even though "Procsimus ardet Eucalygon," no one troubles his head about insurance up here. Our nearest white neighbours are a colony of gum-diggers, at the Kaiwaka swamp, two miles lower down the river; they have built quite a little village of these "nekau" huts, and live a most celibate life, for I don't think there is a woman in the settlement. They generally work in parties of four and five, taking it in turn to remain at home to do the cooking, or scrape the gum clean which has been brought in the previous day. The first time I saw them at work with their gum-spears, they puzzled me as much as I did my brother when he saw me stirring the porridge with the handle of a large wooden rake in default of a spoon, as he came up the river one day. The " spear" is simply a spike of iron, about a foot long, on the end of a pole, with which they " prick" the ground where the kauri gum is found. Directly they hear the iron ring, they dig round the spot and find a lump of gum, generally about nine inches beneath the surface. I think it brings twenty shillings a hundredweight on the spot, after being cleaned; but they have to pay the Maories a royalty of five shillings, which reduces their profits. If a man hits on a good "pocket" of gum, he may make five or six pounds a week; but *au contraire*, for weeks together he scarcely fills the sack on his back. The gum is used in England and America for carriage varnish; and the children about here make very pretty little ornaments from it, much like clear transparent amber, with occasionally a flaky white cloud in the centre. It cuts easily with a knife; and after carving it into a heart, cross, or what not, you rub it with oil and wash-leather before giving it a final polish with kerosene to remove any scratches on the surface. The most curious fact about it is, that for miles and miles there is not a single kauri pine now standing on the gum-fields; you sometimes see gigantic trunks lying across the swamps, half buried in the mud, and in a semi-petrified state, but no live trees are to be seen in the proximity. The theory of the deposits is that in the active volcanic period of New Zealand, these immense forests must have been kindled by the red-hot scoriæ which fell over the country, and that during the conflagration the liquid gum ran into the ground and solidified. Certainly wherever you find a "hummock" of fern and earth, covering an old trunk, you are almost sure to strike "gum" on the lower side of the hill, close beneath the tree. Both the wood and the fossil gum make splendid fuel. I have often crept out of my tent on a drenching wet morning to light a fire in the "open," and cook an early breakfast, with a sense of despondency at successive failures with the damp wood, until one fine day some one suggested making a blaze with a lump of "kauri gum." It burns like turpentine, and with the protection of a bank of sods at the back of my fire-place, and a sheet of corrugated iron to keep the "heavy wet" off, till I got a fair start, I used to triumph over all weathers. There was however a great feeling of relief at seeing our own "store" completed, with a good roomy chimney, across which I could hang my kettle and keep a constant supply of hot water for wet and hungry wayfarers to make their tea or cocoa with. They installed me as cook, and I found that my old experience as a fag at Eton came in very useful to me. The worst of it was, that at school I had all the materials to my hand, and some variety in the dishes; but here, one had to make the bread as well as toast it; and also to bear patiently the muttered complaints of the men, as they saw the eternal junk of salt beef, backed by sardines, potatoes, and even ship-biscuits, appear at every meal. Every Sunday we managed to get enough pigeons and ducks to make a "sea-pie;" and as some of my readers may not understand its mysteries, I shall give them the recipe, for the chance of their ever being similarly circumstanced. You take a good sized iron pot, and put successive layers of paste, potatoes, and meat till full, topping up with paste; of course there must be a little fat and some water to make the gravy, and onions, if you have them; then you stew gently for about three quarters of an hour, and a most savoury mess is produced, fit for the table of Belshazzar or the Emperor Heliogabalus.

My expedients were becoming well-nigh exhausted at last, and I felt like a fellow-passenger of mine between Melbourne and Adelaide, who said, as we leaned over the stern in Lacepede Bay, and looked at the fish darting about, Well! now *if* we could get a bit of fat, we might fry some of those fish, *if* we had 'em!

But at last I resolved, as Mr. Dombey urged his wife, to "make an effort." We sent for two fat sheep from Auckland, which duly arrived in the cutter, and which, though costing the enormous sum of thirty-two shillings each, actually realised a handsome profit retail at the extortionate price (for the colony) of sixpence a pound. To my intense delight also, as I walked across country one evening, I lighted upon a bank of the most beautiful mushrooms, with pink centres and creamy white tops, which I seized upon instanter, and carried carefully home. About the same time, our friends had sent us a box from England, with a number of little delicacies, which can only be prized as they deserve when at such a distance from civilisation. They shall have a treat at last, thought I, instead of the "toujours sardines" diet, to which they have so long submitted; and accordingly, on this occasion, "the Soyer of the camp" out-did himself. I annex the bill of fare:

Julienne Soup, made from little preserved squares, and sent in the box from home.
Roast leg of mutton, fried potatoes, and mushrooms.
Stewed prunes and figs, with rice.
Candied ginger.
Tea and cocoa, dried for a quarter of an hour before the fire, to bring out the flavour before mixing.

We also unpacked our cask of crockery, and enjoyed our China tea-cups, saucers, plates, etc., like Christians, instead of feeding from those horrible tin pannikins and dishes.

The only rebuffs I encountered were that my scullery-man, like King Alfred, let the cakes, or rather rice, burn; and one of the "hands," a canny old Scotchman, objected to "thae puddock-stools," which I had stewed with butter and flour in my most artistic style.

It was not long before I got a cow and calf to these remote parts, to supplement my kitchen with a dairy; but "thereby hangs a tale," which I reserve for another chapter. The only drawback to our table was the want of milk, though, if I had had all my wits about me, I might have brought up some tins of the condensed milk from town. There were many charms about this semi-savage life; among the greatest was the utter absence of conventionalities; no tall black hats ("bell-toppers," à la coloniale), no gloves, no stiff shirt-collars, even no coats on a hot day; and then, in the mornings, when you woke with the fresh air of summer breathing gently in at the open door of the tent (for it hardly ever blows hard between five and eight a.m.), you had but a few yards to walk from your bed, and, with one plunge, were swimming in the cool waters of the Kaihu river, which ran so alluringly close at hand. People often talk of the rapid spread of the Anglo-Saxon race, and, when discussing its greatness, wonder what signs of it will be left thousands of years hence, should the race itself have disappeared. Most observers would say that future generations of men will trace our power and genius by the Cyclopean embankments and cuttings, which a spider-like net of railroads is forming over the face of the habitable globe; but here in New Zealand, at least, three infallible witnesses will be found to attest our influence. I never rowed up a creek or back-water, in the most secluded part of the native country, without finding an empty black beer-bottle from Tennant's Lady Well Brewery, Glasgow, bobbing in the water; and I never crossed a flat, or any large tract of bush, without seeing a sardine-tin, or an abandoned paper-collar, slowly settling down in the dust, to puzzle the Lyells, and Lubbocks, and Murchisons of a later day, when, in company with Macaulay's New Zealander, they visit the shores of England, and find similar deposits there in the strata of the present epoch.

After the men had stopped work, eaten their supper, and lit their pipes, my brother or myself, after drawing up to the fire our arm-chair (extemporised from a hip-bath, with a pillow at the bottom of it), used to read aloud to them for an hour or two before we went to bed. A good many of them had never seen Dickens' works; and when we began "Martin Chuzzlewit," you might have heard a pin drop in the old cook-house. Every now and then they would give vent to their feelings, with an audible expression about "that brute Pecksniff, serve him right;" or a pitying shake of the head, as I read of Jonas Chuzzlewit's brutality to his wife. I almost frightened myself the night we got to that chapter about the murder of Mr. Montagu; the wind whistled so gloomily round our wooden house, and just as we came to the most horrible part of the story, the sheet of corrugated iron which served us for a door fell in with a crash, and a blast of cold air came rushing through the aperture, as we jumped from our seats with scared faces to look what had happened.

But there are no ghosts in New Zealand; the country is not old enough for such "sensations;" so we soon subsided into our beds, and slept as only those wearied with honest manual labour in the finest climate in the world can sleep.

We think of building a house for the manager, up beyond a settlement called Taita, where the chief Te Roore lives; the spot we are likely to choose is near the old ruins of the Mission-station, where Mr. Buller used to live. The stream is fringed with willows, the banks are far out of the reach of floods; and, as far as the eye can reach, is a fertile flat of Phormium and peach trees, from which last the Maories used to bring us "kits" of delicious fruit the first summer we spent up here.

Since T—— left me alone in my glory, I have had many queer experiences. I went down to see him off by the "Pai-Marire" cutter, which derives its name from the Hauhau motto (Peace, be still), and found that my horse "Taffy" had arrived by that mail, with the cow and calf, which I had been anxiously waiting for, to inaugurate my dairy arrangements. My brother rather laughed at the idea of getting the trio of quadrupeds overland that night, through a meshwork of bush and swamps, which was puzzling enough in broad daylight; but I resolved to make the attempt. Having got the assistance of one of our boatmen, off we started about four o'clock, and in a very few minutes our troubles began; the calf wouldn't be driven at all; the cow kept running off the track, even after I had slung the calf across the horse's back to attract her maternal instincts; but at last we devised a plan which promised every prospect of success. One of us mounted the horse and drove the cow; the other tied a rope to the calf, which ran after its mother. Whenever the cow turned off the road, we checked the calf till we drove her back, and she never went far without it. So, by slow stages, we surmounted our difficulties until we had reached our southern boundary line, the Maungatāra Creek, where, as dusk fell, we entered Puhi's swamp, which was pretty familiar ground. But alas! I was no better than a child when darkness came on; I lost my bearings directly, and that infernal cow kept trotting off into soft places where my horse sank to the girths, if I attempted to follow. At last, about fifty yards from the further side of the swamp, we both fairly gave in; and, leaving the cow hopelessly bogged, I took the horse to the edge, and tethered him to some ti-tree. We then went back, and dragged the other poor beast out by her tail and horns, as she moaned helplessly, and placed her on a little island of tussock grass, where we secured the calf to a flax bush. Next morning I found her lying exhausted in exactly the same place where I had left her the previous night; and it took an hour and a half to haul her on to dry land, across that little bit of a bog. I never tried this amusement again, but drove her right round the head of the swamps, and nearly over to the sea-coast, which, though it trebled the distance, was a far more simple task. But to return to where I left the horse. After mounting the hill, the sky became overcast, and, for the first time in my experience, I was utterly and entirely "lost in the bush." It was no good walking further, for we had no idea in what direction we were moving, so we sat down in the darkness for the morn to rise. Presently we began to feel thirsty; but before we dare stir to look for water, we lit the bushes for a beacon to guide us on our return. After a long search, stumbling over "pockets," from which kauri gum had been dug, and which are very awkward for a careless rider, we found a few small holes of rain-water, which gave us enough to wet our lips; and then, after smoking our pipes in sullen silence for a time at our wood fire, the Southern Cross suddenly peeped out, and the moon broke out from the bank of clouds on the horizon. I then recollected that if I could strike the native track to the west coast, and follow it along, I should find a newspaper flag on the bushes, which would give me the direct line for turning off home. We soon succeeded in our search, and arrived at the mill about half-past eleven at night. It was very fortunate that my brother had thought of tying up these landmarks of paper as we were exploring short cuts over our block of land, as in daylight we could see them a quarter of a mile away; and by constantly making a bee line for them, and chopping here and there a ti-tree to guide us in between, we soon established a well-defined track on the nearest and best line of march.

We used to find it hardest to prevent circling round and round when cutting a road in the forest, for then one had no view ahead; but the compass afforded some assistance; and we could also start from different sides, giving an occasional call, as we neared each other, to see if we were going straight. I could never resist slicing off the head of a "nekau-palm" as I passed, if it looked particularly tempting; for the white succulent flesh of the young leaves is very like celery in consistency and taste. I think it quite possible that we shall make some use, too, of the leaves of the cabbage-tree (what Lady Barker calls the ti-tree *palm*); the fibre is very strong and clean, but short; and requires boiling to get rid of the green outer coating.

What puzzles one most in our amateur road-making, is the way in which the face of the country alters in the wet season; where we walked dry-shod the other day, we find next week either a treacherous bog, or else it is chest deep in water; and I have had one short acquaintance with a summer "fresh," that is vividly impressed on my memory still. There had been three months of consecutive sunshine, and we had stacked our timber for the mill, close to where it was landed, in apparent safety. The rain came at last without any previous warning; and for three days we had an unceasing down-pour. The first night made me take to the "store," for I had the weather-side of the tent, and after a vain attempt to sleep in my mackintosh, I found the insidious drip and patter from the roof was sure to creep in at some weak or exposed corner, and give one a cold shiver as it trickled down the body.

During the next two days the river kept rising rapidly, for the dry ground was unable to drink in the rain fast enough owing to the previous drought, which had caked it so hard; and all the surface drainage ran off at once as from a duck's back. I felt uneasy the third day, when the water had reached the level of the banks, and sat up measuring its rise, which was at the rate of an inch every half hour. I carried the bulletins to the tent, where one of my companions still held out bravely; and after my repeated warnings had wakened him from an incipient drowse into a state of the most fidgety watchfulness, he at last sprang to his feet, with an exclamation of "Here it comes through the tent!" We carried all our possessions up the hill side, and out of harm's way; and then, at two a.m., worked hard to remove our timber to a safe distance, splashing about in the overflow which had already reached the stack. It was only after having to "turn" out like this, or when one had passed a restless night with other little torments, which abound in newly-cleared places, that I ever regretted the luxuries of a town, or thought that I had bragged a little too much of the "glorious liberty" of bush-life.

"Romæ Tibur amem, ventoso Tibure Romam" is a far truer remark than most of us think; and I am afraid, at this distance, I think only of the delights of that life; but if boating on that lovely river, and breathing that pure air, was pleasant to me after coming from Oxford, where our Nuneham water-parties at Commemoration time had the additional charms of female society, and other creature comforts that were missing here, what must such a life appear to a working-man from the old country? There he probably tastes meat but seldom; he undergoes real hardships, in a miserable climate, and on stinted wages; but here, one of our "hands" actually grumbled because he could only lay by fourteen shillings out of his thirty shillings a-week. On a wet day I have known the boatmen refuse to turn out and brave the inclemency of the day, and leave us ourselves to carry the mails down to Mangawhare, whilst they did a "government stroke," and lolled in their huts over a pipe. Any labourer who can pay his passage out to New Zealand is a fool to remain at home; for here he feels himself almost on equal terms with the man of capital, and has him almost at his mercy. So far from losing in social advantages by the change, as an educated gentleman may do, he makes a positive gain in this respect; and, if he is only fairly steady and saving, may realise a position which he could never attain to in older countries, where the laws of caste and prejudice are so tyrannical in their operation. "Slow rises worth, by poverty oppressed," may be true of England; but in America or New Zealand, a poor man, who will not loaf or be ashamed of manual labour, is bound to get on well.

We have already built seven cottages for our workmen, which they occupy free of rent; and they are quite at liberty to enclose a piece of land for garden produce, which begins to give a ship-shape appearance to Katangi, our first village.

I rather enjoy christening the new spots with old and well-remembered names from home; for instance, we intend to pick out a site for "Aigburth" settlement, if enough people would come out from Liverpool to entitle it to the name; and I think myself it removes the feeling of exile, which emigrants experience on first reaching their adopted country, to find familiar names already planted there. T——, however, is inclined to adopt the rule of retaining Maori names, wherever they are really poetical and decent (many being quite unfit for translation), which would not leave much room for my scheme. It adds very much to this same illusion, if all the settlers bring a few flowerseeds from home to scatter broadcast in this flowerless island. Though the ferns and creepers are so exquisite in their variety, I know of only two flowers, the Rata and the Phormium, which shine out conspicuously with their scarlet or crimson blossoms from an all-pervading green. I have sown a little packet of cowslips near the mill already; and I fully intend that, before many years elapse, the country under our care shall be covered with daisies, primroses, and heather each returning spring. Everything that grows at home should grow still better here, if I am not mistaken; and it would be a real delight to find violets and lily-of-the-valley in the "bush," whilst the more domestic roses and carnations lent a novel brightness to the house-front. It is not much use to attempt a vegetable garden, until we get a strong enclosure built to keep out the pigs,—not the wild pigs, but an impudent little porker, called Tommy, which our friend Parore gave us when calling one day. He is provokingly tame; but as he does not "pay the rint" like Paddy's pig, we occasionally come to loggerheads, when I find him rooting up my turnips, or invading the sacred precincts of the "store," where he sometimes steals a surreptitious doze, nestled in a heap of shavings. Often when we are out walking, he will follow us for miles like a dog; and I could never make up my mind to kill him, even when at the last extremities for fresh meat. What can one do, when he confides so securely in your honour? It is impossible to strike the fatal blow! as he trots off to your side, with a plaintive grunt, to wish you good morning.

I had sowed four beds of vegetables, viz., turnips, cabbage, cauliflowers, and radishes, but only the first and last made their appearance. The ground requires a good deal of preparation besides digging over; all the fern-root should be picked out and burnt, or it sours and impoverishes the soil to such an extent that your crops can make no head.

This district of the North Wairoa however, will some day be the fruit country and vineyard of the two islands. The grapes are really magnificent, and peaches, though of course hardly equal to hot-house and wall-fruits, surpass the flavourless productions which they "can," or preserve, in the United States. I have seen cumeras (sweet potatoes) as large as a man's head; and all this, remember, under Maori cultivation, which is of the most meagre description. You often hear people say in jest, of very prolific lands, that if you "tickle the earth, she smiles with crops"; but here the proverb is literally true, for the natives scarcely scratch up three inches of the surface.

The other day, when we were invited to "lunch" at Parore's, he gave us a vegetarian entertainment of cumeras, calabash and taro. I don't think either of the latter grow in the South Island. The taro is the great staple of food with the Kanakas of Honolulu, and, in fact, all the inhabitants of the Pacific. It requires copious irrigation; its leaf is not unlike that of a water lily, but the flower is a bright pink, and the edible bulb or root is of a lilac colour, and tastes a little like a yam, but the substance is stickier and more glutinous. I always thought it best when cut into slices, and baked like "scones," or potato-cakes.

We have seen a good deal of Maori customs lately, and I suppose that, as we have come to reside in the neighbourhood, they look upon us as members of the "hapu," or family connection, and pay us ceremonious calls, much as you would to new arrivals in England. The first visit we had was from Maria, a "chiefess," who owns most of the estate on which we live. She is a pleasant, dignified woman, about thirty, and the most industrious native I have seen. Whether in a canoe or on horseback, or while chatting to us, she has perpetually got a piece of knitting or needlework in hand. She took a very intelligent interest in our mills, and put a leaf of Phormium through the dressing-machine with her own hands. Of course it did not come out as white or silky as what she herself could have prepared with the pipi-shell; but the rapidity of our process amazed her, and also the fact that we utilised the whole leaf; whereas in hand-dressing nearly two-thirds of the fibre are left in and wasted. When the inspection was concluded, she sent us a present of a basket of tairoas, a large white shell-fish from the coast, which is considered a delicacy by those who can't get oysters. The natives find them by digging in the sand wherever they see a breathing-hole; and when roasted, or, better still, made into soup, they are not unlike the clams of New England.

Parore's son rowed up to lunch a few days after Maria had been here, and amused us a good deal by his attempts to handle a knife and fork, which he had never seen before. He held them with his fist clenched, which gave him more strength than delicacy of manipulation; and, as he refused advice, and would not use his fingers, it took him some time to finish his food.

The most important and interesting ceremonial, however, that took place while I was there, was a "huhunga," or bone-scraping, at which nearly four hundred Maories were present. You must know, that after a body has been buried some two years, the remains are disinterred, and the bones carefully scraped. The latter are then wrapped up in a new blanket or shawl, and sent off to their relatives, who deposit the precious relics in some hiding place, known only to a select few. This precaution is taken to prevent insult after death by enemies of the deceased or his tribe; and one frequently comes across such "chapels of bones" in the most remote corners and caves of the country.

As I walked up to Taita, where the family gathering was to be, I noticed casually that nearly all the large puriri-trees had marks of the tomahawk on them, and the only explanation I could suggest was, that the surveyors had chipped out the pieces to make them serve as land-marks; but we afterwards heard that there is a grub which buries itself in the trunk, and that here, as in Australia, it is considered a great delicacy by the native gourmands, whose mouths water on extracting the savoury morsel, much as ours might do over a Whitstable "native," or a creamy "Saddle-Rock" oyster from New York; and with equally good reason too, allowing for the difference of tastes.

When nearing the village, I picked up a skin of the original black rat, "a thing of which you often read, very seldom see;" for he has been nearly exterminated, or eaten out of house and home, by his brown brothers from Norway. I have been told that no such animal exists now; but here was evidence to the contrary. It had been cleanly skinned from the carcase, as if with a knife, by the "more-pork," a small owl which preys on such vermin, and which gets its name from the melancholy and monotonous cry it utters through the night.

The fur of the rat was of a glossy black, but the longer hairs were tipped with grey, rather like a baby 'possum skin from Tasmania. I tried hard to keep it a curiosity; but having no means of preserving it at hand, I had to throw it away before I got back, to prevent it walking off itself.

Taita, the Maori settlement to which I was going, is picturesquely situated on a small peninsula, between two tributaries of the Kaihu, across which lie natural rustic bridges, formed of single totara pines, which the natives have felled across the stream. The size of these trees may be estimated, when I say that a horse can easily walk over them from end to end as they lie. The sight which greeted me, as I entered the enclosure, was sufficiently quaint. In the centre of the stockade was a group of "tamariki," or children, playing at cricket with the most primitive bats in the world; at the further end of the enclosure hung two bundles of red blanket, swinging in the breeze, which contained the bones of two distinguished strangers, whose friends had come to convey them to their last resting-place.

I found Te Roore's whare or hut, full of notable chiefs from Hokianga and the Bay of Islands, to whom I was introduced as "the most recent addition to the 'hapu,' or social circle of Kaihu Valley." The lady of the house soon made her appearance, and, seizing my hands in her own (which were rather sticky, from eating dried eels and decomposed shark's fin), exclaimed, Tenakoe (*You* here? which is the Maori How d' ye do?) then, after a pause, Tena-a-a-akoe (What? *you* here, this is indeed an honour, I feel much flattered by your condescension, etc.), and then a long-drawn breath, Eh-h-h! confirmation of the above. Whilst they sent off for their interpreter, Te Roore (a finished diplomatist, by-the-bye, who is famed far and wide for his silvery laugh) pressed upon me rum and biscuits, apologising for the absence of fish. Presently, they returned with the object of their search; a white man, named Tom Johnston, who is living here with another lad, and has married a native wife. He does their fencing, etc., and often has to go and catch eels in the evening, while the chiefs recline at ease in their blankets waiting for supper. Rather a servile office, considering our received opinions of the respective position dark and light skins should hold with regard to each other.

Separated from the rest of the inhabitants, and in a state of "Coventry," were the bone-scrapers, who had performed the last offices to the dead. These wretched men are not allowed to touch food or anything else with their fingers for some days after the pollution; but are fed with long sticks, from which they gnaw the meat or potatoes, like so many brute beasts. It is a pitiable and disgusting sight; but the Maoris have the strictest possible rules of "tapu" on such an occasion, and would never think of using any utensil again if it came in contact with these fellows.

There are two customs, or superstitions, which are a constant source of difficulty to strangers here, viz., the "tapu," or consecration, and the "utu," or forfeiture. Quite lately I was bringing a heavy barge up the river, and, having got it about half way before the turn of tide, was about to moor it for the night to a willow, which stood near Puhi's house. To my surprise, the boatmen begged me not to do this, for the tree had been "tapued" by Puhi, and anything tied to it would be claimed by him, if we broke the "tapu." The forfeiture of a person's effects, or "utu," is generally for more serious offences, such as adultery or homicide, in which the injured individual lays his case before a meeting of the tribe, and they decide to what extent he may mulct the offender, by taking his horse and saddle or requiring a money-payment as a fine.

I would refer anyone who is curious on these points to a very amusing book, the *Pakeha Maori*, by Judge Manning, who lives at Hokianga, about two days' journey north of us. He has been for thirty years living among these people, and his "mana" or influence, is said to be very great with them.

At all important meetings, they have a custom of presenting kits of potatoes, biscuits, &c., to all who attend. The quantity and quality of the "backsheesh" varies according to your rank. I dare say R——, one of the Lands' court judges, whose jurisdiction as magistrate I dare say extends over nearly two hundred square miles, would receive two canoe-loads of provisions, if he came to a "bone-scraping" in his official capacity, or as a dignitary of the county.

When potatoes were selling at extortionate prices in Auckland, and it even paid our merchants to import them in steamers from Sydney; when, also, the poorer natives were starving from the failure of the crops, or begging for Government rations, Parore would frequently pay us a visit at the Mill, and bring a present of half-a-dozen kits from his ample store of perquisites, as one of the Ngapuhi chiefs.

When I entered the village of Taita, I found a warm discussion going on about our "lease;" and, at the risk of being tedious, I must explain somewhat of our local politics.

Our land forms about a quarter of a very fertile block, called the Kaihu Valley, the whole of which (about two hundred thousand acres) the Provincial Government have been trying to buy for years, for the purpose of forming a special settlement. There is this difficulty, however, about the purchase. Land is not owned here by individuals, but by the whole tribe; and this particular piece belongs jointly to the Ngapuhis and the Uriohaus. Until they decide among themselves to arrange the boundaries, and also to "individualise" their titles, it is hard to know who is entitled to receive the payment. We have at present a body of ten landlords, all of whom receive a portion of the

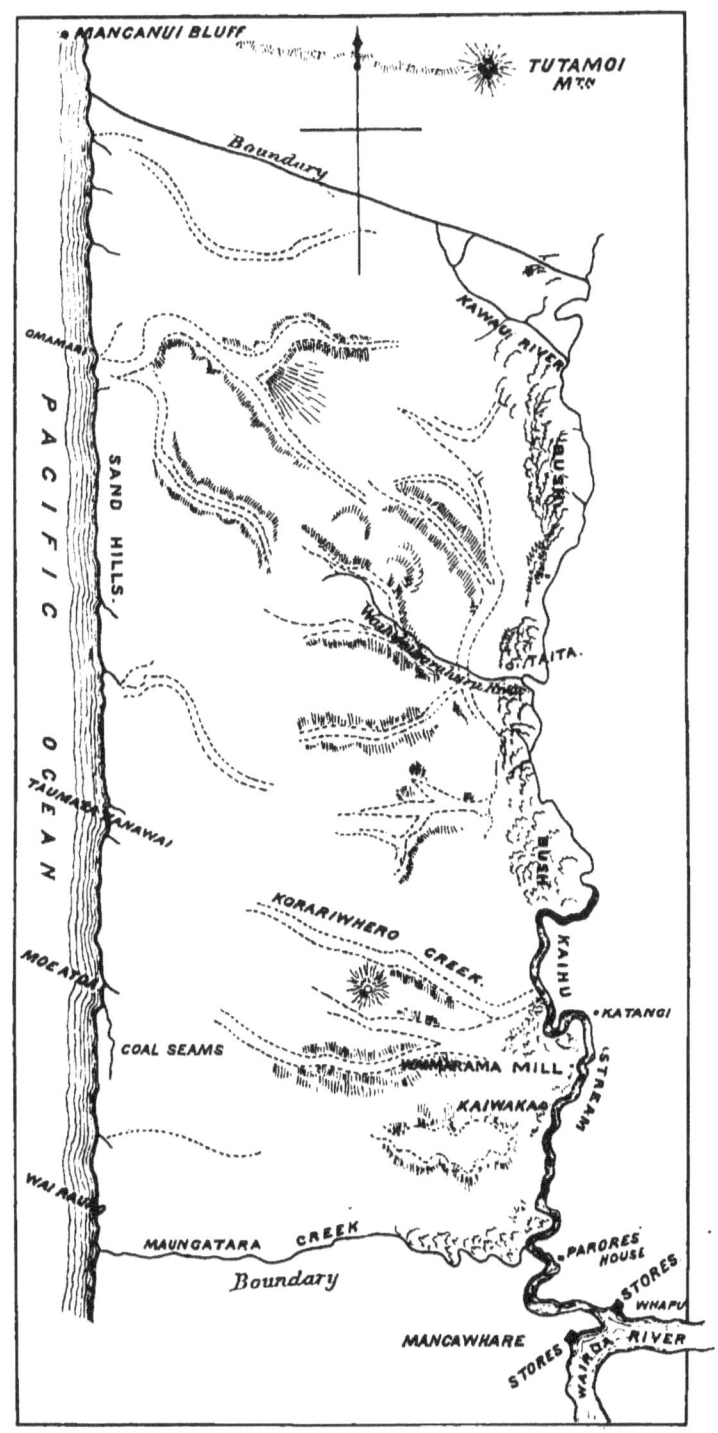

PLAN OF KAIHU ESTATE.

rent, on behalf of their still more numerous clients, who established their claims to a share of it, as follows ;—The lands' court gave notice, that it was agreed to lease a piece of land to us, and that, by a certain date, all claimants to the property must register their titles before they could receive a grant from the Crown as landlords.

All sorts of the most absurd reasons were advanced, according to the usual custom, by the representatives of these two tribes, as well as others from outlying districts, to establish their rights.

For instance, one man recollected landing, five years ago, to cook his food as he passed up the river; and the ashes of his fire, if they could be found, must be conclusive evidence of his occupancy. Another had eaten a piece of some celebrated warrior there, after a fight in the neighbourhood; and a title dating from the good old days of cannibalism was surely indefeasible. A third had hunted wild pigs; a fourth had thrown some peach-stones ashore, which must have become trees by this time, and you could hardly deny him his tenant-right or compensation, for had he not improved the value of the land by this scientific fruit-culture, extending over the laborious term of five seconds?

Such were some of the stories which judicial patience had to sift before we received a legal document, stating exactly to whom we were indebted for the amount of our annual rent.

When the deed was signed, Tirarau, a great potentate from the North Wairoa, made a congratulatory address to the other natives, stating that, as they had been brought into one enclosure (the lease), he hoped the close quarters would conduce to the settlement of all outstanding feuds. My brother had gone up to witness the signatures; and he told me that at the conclusion of this speech the whole audience suddenly retired to their huts, and reappeared again in a costume that would not pass muster in Regent Street. They had taken off every stitch of clothing, with the exception of a girdle round the waist; one exquisite had wrapped the Union Jack round his middle; and all had clubbed-muskets in their hands. He felt somewhat nervous as they rushed towards him with a kind of hoarse shout; but they stopped short within a few yards, and began a real war-dance in honour of the occasion, keeping the most mechanical and exact time in their movements. You may talk of animated clock-work or Marionettes; but here, the rolling eyes, protruded tongues, and panting gasp at intervals, gave a hideous expression to the performers, which would frighten a child out of his wits; whilst the peculiar agility displayed throughout the entertainment reminded one strongly of the song about "a yaller-girl a-kicking up behind and before."

I don't think this dispute about the ownership of the Kaihu Valley will ever do *us* any harm; the natives may fight each other, but would hardly be so stupid as to drive us away and lose their source of income. The dispute I myself heard when up at Taita was more especially about the question of "burnt flax." They had specified in the lease that, for every hundred acres of Phormium destroyed by gum-diggers when clearing the ground, we should be excused £100 per annum of the rent. When we held back this amount at the quarter-day, the Uriohaus turned sulky, and said that, as all the burning had taken place in a swamp of Parore's, it was only fair that his tribe, the Ngapuhis, should suffer the loss, whilst they received their full share of the rent. I don't know how they settled it; but we paid in the full amount owing to their duly-appointed agent at Mangawhare, and left him to divide it as best he could.

There is, however, a far more serious question looming in the future, and one which Tamati Waka, an old and trusty friend of the white man, is confident will breed trouble (and possibly war) with the colonists. It is the "Surplus Lands Act." In days gone by, when the natives bartered their land away for a mere song, kegs of nails or axes were often enough, in the hands of a cunning settler, to secure a block of eight thousand acres, or more.

When, however, a paternal government, which was not itself ashamed to bamboozle the Maoris into the treaty of Waitangi, ceding the sovereignty of the islands to Queen Victoria, came to scrutinise these early transactions between individual white men and their new subjects, it decided, with gross injustice to both alike, that no white man *could* purchase more than (say) four thousand acres in his own name; and that therefore all surplus lands, even though bought under the old régime, must pass to Government, not (mark you) to their original possessors, the Maoris. Now what the latter say, is: "If we were robbed or cheated of our land from ignorance, and you decide to deprive the purchasers of their bargain, it should belong to us again, and not to you. You pretend to be acting in our interests, but really are robbing both parties."

It is very like the fable of the lawyer, who swallowed the oyster, and left the disputants the two empty shells.

As I sauntered back from Taita to Mangawhare, I thought what a much happier life half the young fellows at home might lead here, instead of being boxed up in those hateful offices all their life, to inhale the grimy air of London with its November fogs, and still more trying heat in the long summer-days, when one longs to leave the four prison-walls of desk routine, and revel in the delight of the country. We have no sallow faces, or narrow chests, or suspicious coughs in the healthy climate of Kaihu. 'Tis true that the pioneer work of a flax-mill elicited a few grumbles from our "hands" at first starting:

"Fortunati nimium, sua si bona nôrint."

But in a couple of months, almost as if by the touch of a magician's wand, the features of the place were transformed. Before we go back, there will be a church and school up at Taita, where Dr. Cowie, Bishop of Auckland, paid his first visit the other day, on a tour through the diocese.

It may be that one forgets the discomforts too easily, and paints a Utopia which does not yet exist; but even in our real misfortunes there was a romantic zest, which robbed them of half their sting. "What fun it will be to talk about this when we see the old folks at home again," is a constant thought of emigrants in their distant exile.

Perhaps our hardest work at the mill was navigating rafts of timber and heavy barges, before we learnt the thousand dangers that beset us from snags, freshes, and tides; for the stream of the Kaihu, though itself quite fresh and fit to drink, is "backed up" by the flow of salt water from Kaipara Harbour. The first adventure of this sort was particularly disagreeable, and enough to dishearten anyone. T—— had brought the first load of machinery up to the mill-site with the tide; and after mooring the punt to the bank, deservedly sought his much-needed rest. When he went down to the river in the morning, he found the punt had hitched on the bank when the tide ran out, and capsized. There lay all our heavy machinery in twelve feet of water, including a ten-horse portable engine, and numerous smaller etcetera.

I should have despaired of recovering it; but T——, who was the only one up there who could dive, set to work at once, and spent a whole day off and on, seated on the mud at the bottom of the stream, and tying ropes to the wheels as he groped along and felt them. He's a most ingenious fellow, and never neglects an opportunity on board ship of learning from the sailors some new "hitch," or "Tartar's head," or some equally mysterious arrangements of the rope, so that one could depend on his knots when he had tied them. He stuck to his task so indefatigably that before night everything was on terrâ firmâ, and we lost nothing but a tin dish, which may have slithered along any distance down the river.

My turn came next, as follows : We started down with the tide at ten p.m. in the heavy barge, to bring up the flax machines and scutches, which had just come round in the schooner from Auckland; and I was steering. I forget whether I was drowsy at having to leave a warm bed at such an uncanny time of night, or whether I was watching the weird blue eyes of phosphoric light in the water, which the Maoris say are those of the taniwha, or monster who devours men. They are dreadfully afraid of this fabulous creature, and you can hardly get them to stir out after dusk, for they see him glaring at them from the eddies of the whirlpool as the canoe passes rapidly by. But whatever my thoughts were, we had made about six miles with the aid of the strong "fresh," and I was congratulating myself that I soon would be warming before a good fire, when suddenly a queer grating sound was heard, as the punt half slid over a hidden snag (which I ought to have known), then swung round to the stream, and finally settled hard and fast in her berth. We rocked her about, and pushed and hauled, but with a rapidly falling tide all our efforts failed to make her budge one inch; so there we were for the night. I wrapped myself in my plaid, lay down on the sloppy planks, and dreamt fitful dreams of home, till I wakened up in the grey dawn to a weary task of rowing the remaining three miles against the tide, whose flow had lifted us off the snag at last.

I was determined to have no more of these midnight plaisanteries; so, as day broke, and the sun rolled back the heavy white banks of fog from the hills, I loaded the old punt at the Kaihu wharf with about ten tons of ironwork, and to within half an inch of her leaky seam through which I could see the ripple of the waves. But, sink or swim, I was determined to take the lot in one trip, and have no further worry. We worked hard on our return, and got up to the mill in one tide; but I was very nervous about another capsize, and moored the punt stem and stern in the middle of the river till next morning. This heavy rowing is not quite congenial to me, after being accustomed to a light gig from Searle's or Salter's; and it cramped my fingers so that I could not close my fist for a full fortnight afterwards; but muscular Christianity, with all its crosses, is better than that perpetual quill-driving, whether it be in law or commerce.

Much as I should like to write something more practical about the Phormium industry before I leave my hobby of "our flax mill," I am afraid to damp the romance of life at Kaihu by statistics and dry facts; but I have gone thus far because so many people have asked me in England, what there is to do in New Zealand besides taking a "sheep station;" for though the "squatters" have their good years, I really don't think many of them clear much money in the long run. Last year, the exceptionally high price of wool brought them on the right side of their bankers' books; but, as a consequence of this, they have doubled the value of their "runs," and a young beginner would find it very hard to buy in now at at all a safe price. Of course, if I were asked about the pleasures of such a life, I should tell any one that, with a good horse, comfortable house and food, all the latest English magazines and papers, and such society as Canterbury Province affords (where every second man is from a first-class English school or University), he must be very exigeant if he were not pleased. A man can have no fairer sketch of both sides of the question, than you find in Lady Barker's *Station Life in New Zealand*. I think, however, that perhaps people starting in this line now would be able to invest their money more economically, by taking up some of the new lands in the Waikato districts of the North Island, where there are no severe winters or snowstorms to kill their flocks, and towards which already a tide is gradually setting of the more adventurous squatters from Canterbury and Otago.

The next and most alluring occupation to new comers who cannot afford a sheep-run is gold mining. I cannot call it an industry, though there is plenty of hard work to be done at the "diggings." What I mean is, that beyond drawing population to uninhabited lands, and benefiting a lucky few, it does no good at all; it rather draws men from permanent and productive industries, which do far more for the country at large. I have been told that every pound's worth of gold from the field costs twenty-five shillings to extract it, if you set the total costs against the total expenses of the diggings. Gold mining is a kind of gambling; and the temporary excitement of a great find like the "Caledonian" at the Thames, where they obtained half a million in two months, seems to set men's minds ablaze. The feeling is as unhealthy for the neighbouring towns, as it is for the individuals actively employed on the spot. Take the case of Auckland: I can almost count on my fingers the men there who confine themselves to steady, commercial work; the rest of the beings, who haunt the

New Exchange or the lower end of Shortland Crescent, are "spiders" or sharebrokers, who make their living by the feverish rise or fall of the market, dependent as it often is on vamped-up reports from Coromandel or Grahamstown, where the favourite mine suddenly turns out to have been "salted" with gold as foreign to the spot as imported diamonds to Arizona. All these fellows manipulate money; but they don't make it.

If a man is fond of city life, which is at best a second-rate imitation of England, he may choose three lines here; either the professional career of a clergyman, doctor, or barrister (and I don't think he would find any special advantages in New Zealand); or secondly, commercial life, where the rivalry is greater than at home, because nearly all are struggling for a name, and few are so established as to feel out of reach of competition; or lastly, engineering. I think the last decidedly affords a good opening at present.

We have borrowed ten millions, of which a great portion will be spent on railroads already surveyed. Coalfields are springing up in myriads; and I saw quite lately specimens, from the Miranda Redoubt, near the Thames, fully equal to the cannel-coal used here in gasworks. The Taranaki iron-sand has been at last actually used, after repeated failures; and there are miles of it on the beach at New Plymouth lying idle yet. In fact, there are few countries so naturally gifted with materials for engineering, and fewer still where such a rife opportunity for their development exists.

Those, however, who prefer the country, and are unable to raise capital enough to "squat" on a sheep-station, where, like the patriarchs of old, they may count their flocks and herds by thousands, would probably choose either a farmer's or a flax-planter's life. Now, *a propos* of the former, I have heard poor people at home run down

the Australian and New Zealand preserved meats, which no doubt may suffer a little from packing and transport; but let me assure them that out in the colony, Invercargill beef, merino mutton from Canterbury, Stilton and Cheshire cheeses made in Rangitikei and the Waikato, can fairly hold their own against anything from the old country. A farmer who is ambitious enough to extend his operations beyond the dairy or root-crops, can now easily find a sale for his "beeves" with the meat-preserving companies, whose trade is assuming proportions beyond all previous expectation. But, in my opinion, the flax-planter's life presents even more attractions than farming, if you look at it from a pecuniary point of view; and it derives an additional interest from the vast number of uses to which the fibre can and will be shortly put by those who are devoting themselves to the industry. The fact that the plant is only found in full perfection in New Zealand, though indigenous also to the Scilly and Channel Islands, makes the manufacture quite a specialty of the colony, which we are wisely taking pains to encourage, by means of premiums, exhibitions, and the labours of a permanent "Flax Commission."

I have heard lately of the erection of immense rope-walks at San Francisco, which will depend to a great extent upon our little island for their material. The supply of Manilla hemp cannot meet the increasing demand at home and abroad for strong fibres, and I confess I heard with selfish satisfaction, the other day, that the crop there this year has been seriously damaged by some little insect, which, from its evident partiality for us, in thus encouraging our Phormium of New Zealand by the destruction of its rival, deserves at once to be idolised like the sacred beetle of the Egyptians, and placed among the household gods of Kaihu.

Among other uses of the flax (not to mention that a mere strip of the green leaf will mend a stirrup-leather or girth, or do for a shoe-lace, more especially if it be slightly heated at the fire first to melt the gum), I found that the refuse, when fresh, is an excellent febrifuge and tonic, with a not unpleasant bitter taste.

But as we seldom get sick in New Zealand, and the medicine would be apt to accumulate on our hands, it is also worth mentioning that, when boiled, it forms a rich brown dye, and in conjunction with the peaty water of swamps, is used to colour the beautiful little hand-bags, kits, and mats, which the natives plait for sale in Auckland and New Plymouth.

Our fibre has already survived the antipathies and jealousies with which manufacturers always regard anything which necessitates a new adaptation of their machinery; it has ceased to fluctuate between extremes in the market, and is now steadily rising in price, as its too little known capabilities become realised at home, whilst in New Zealand the first "rush" into the new industry has slackened; and instead of clergymen, schoolmasters, and small capitalists with less knowledge than capital, who burnt their fingers over this, as their prototypes did in the first days of the railway mania at home, we have now men of experience and energy, and sufficiently prudent to maintain a uniform standard of excellence in their shipments, which of itself will materially develop the trade in our new "staple."

THE KAWAU.

ABOUT twenty-eight miles to the N.E. of Auckland, in the Hauraki Gulf, there is a little island called the Kawau, which brings back vividly to one's memory the tales one has read in boyhood of fairy spots in the Pacific seas, where cast-away mariners, like Robinson Crusoe, used to live in solitary glory. Just as the Earls of Derby ruled the Isle of Man in olden days, or Mr. Augustus Smith more recently the Scilly Islands, so at the Kawau Sir George Grey, the former Governor of New Zealand, is absolute

> " Monarch of all he surveys,
> And his right there is none to dispute."

This island, which measures about thirty miles round, contains three magnificent harbours, one of which could easily float the *Great Eastern* close to the shore at low water. As you enter the middle harbour in the *Comerang*, a Bay of Islands' steamer, which calls in with the weekly mail from Auckland, a large English-looking house suddenly breaks upon the sight from a lovely sequestered bay to the right, where it stands embosomed in trees, within a few yards of the shelving beach of white sand and gravel. The loud whistle of the boat wakens the echoes of the hills and glens as she nears the long pier, from which a little boat is already putting out, laden with produce for the Auckland market, and expectant of the newspapers and letters which link their quiet existence with the busy stir and bustle of the great outside world.

And this is indeed a spot where one might be well

contented to pass the remainder of one's life in blissful tranquillity; amid scenes of exquisite beauty, with every variety of plant, bird and beast; an almost perfect climate; and a complete absence of care, were it not for the ever-present thought that such an existence is almost too happy for mortal man to lead; it is so completely shut off from human misery that one begins almost to think the tales of poverty in great cities, with their increasing myriads of hunger-stricken squalid beings, are but an ugly dream of the past; for

> "Segnius irritant animum demissa per aurem,
> Quam quæ sunt oculis submissa fidelibus."

This must surely be the Atlantis of the ancients, where the earth gives forth her choicest fruits unasked, where animal life has found its utmost limits of variety and health, and where, with Plato, we may at length find perfect happiness in the contemplation of beauty, and sympathize with nature in her divinest guise.

Before I tell of all the delights of this little Paradise, a type of what New Zealand will become in future years, when her lifeless plains are peopled, her willing soil is planted, and her forests of endless green diversified with the bright colouring of English flowers, let me attempt a short sketch of the previous history of the island.

There is immense interest here for the geologist, both in the mineral riches of the place, and also in the fact that the Kawau is a relic of a far older country than New Zealand. The former has sunk into the sea, for the valleys that still intersect it were clearly, in a previous age, the beds of large rivers, whose watershed must have been from a far wider area than this; whilst the present main-land of New Zealand is still slowly rising from the deep, and thus differs widely from the Kawau in its origin and present state of volcanic disturbance. In fact, so comparatively new a creation are the two islands of New Zealand proper, that it has been frequently remarked that they were inhabited centuries too soon. In the South the glacier period is still grinding down the huge snow-clad mountains and forming of the débris plains for future cultivation; the precise action is there still in force, which men of science detect in the boulders of Huelgoat in Brittany, or those of Wales. The North Island for many square miles is yet a seething and boiling mass of chemical disturbance. The volcano of Tongariro, the earthquakes at Wellington, the hot lakes and geysers of Rotomahana, the extinct crater of Rangitoto at the entrance to the Waitemata or Auckland harbour, whose eruption still lives in Maori tradition, all prove how comparatively recent an addition to our globe this portion of its surface has been. The only land which can compare with the Kawau for antiquity is Karewa Rock, from which Captain Mair lately sent to the British Museum two lizards (Hatteria punctata, Tuatara in Maori), the venerable representatives of an extinct fossil genus found only in that locality.

The Kawau in olden times was inhabited by a population of about two thousand Maories, which proves the fertility of the soil; the adjacent fisheries must also have contributed largely to their sustenance. Now—there is not a living native on the island!

I believe it was bought originally by squatters in New South Wales, who intended to breed stock there. They actually despatched a cargo of beasts, which were landed, but next morning had disappeared in the dense bush, and now form the herd of wild cattle, which infest the forests, and number about five hundred head.

After this, it became the property of a succession of copper-mining companies, who worked to more or less profit the very rich mine on the west side, until in 1849 a discovery of gold in California, and the "rush" to that country deprived them of the necessary labour; and since that time I believe nothing has been done in this direction, although the old shaft and a fine smelting house still remain as evidence of the past enterprise.

Lastly it passed into the hands of its present possessor, Sir George Grey, who is rapidly converting it, by the assistance of his own taste and the natural capabilities of the place, into the Utopia which I am about to describe.

The house is built almost entirely of materials taken from the spot; there are fine kauri forests which supplied timber for the ceiling and walls of the rooms, whilst the matting for the floors is plaited from the native flax (Phormium Tenax), of which vast quantities are found in the swamps of the island.

To show how many-sided an existence one may lead in this retirement, and how one is not entirely dependent on nature here for enjoyment, I may mention that the library contains about the finest collection of works on the dialects of South Africa to be found in the world. They were collected chiefly while Sir G. Grey was Governor of the Cape.

In addition to this, you might spend weeks over his Maori antiques and curiosities, many of them presents from personal friends among his former subjects, and others of them trophies of the last war.

There is the original idol which was brought in the canoes from Hawaii, when the natives colonised New Zealand, made from a hard red stone, for which one may search their present country in vain; there is the wooden flute of the poet Toutanikai; there are also several mere-meres or greenstone clubs, of immense antiquity, the symbols of authority and long descent, every one of which with its minutest flaws is as well known to the Maories as our celebrated diamonds to an expert in jewels. The greenstone itself resembles the Chinese jade, and is only found near Hokitika, on the West Coast of the Middle Island, at the bottom of rivers. It is extremely hard to cut, being of a greasy tough substance, but may be bought in the rough for a mere song. It is seldom that a piece of it turns out well in the cutting. There are two main varieties, the dark opaque and the light semi-transparent, of which the latter appears to be the least common, though perhaps not the most valued. Each great mere has a history of its own, telling who were its possessors, in what battles they had been engaged, how many skulls it had cleft in twain, besides personal anecdotes of the combatants and their families. You may buy a pendant of this stone for your watch-chain at any shop in Auckland for a few shillings; but attempt to bargain with a native lady for the ugly little idol that hangs round her neck, with huge eyes of red sealing-wax, or the lump of greenstone tied in her ear, and at once you find that "thereby hangs a tale," and that the prestige of antiquity has trebled or quadrupled the value of such ornaments. I saw lately the mere of a celebrated chief, named Jaketai, who died in Hawke's Bay Province. His child being still of tender years, the guardians brought the precious heirloom to a friend of mine, and deposited it with him for safety till the rightful heir came of age. As C—— was about to visit England, he asked permission to take the mere with him, which was granted. They however would not touch or look at it themselves when he removed it from the chest where he had kept it, for "was it not 'tapu,' or sacred for a term of years"? He even told me that Jaketai's widow, having caught an accidental glimpse of the club as he was packing it, rushed from the house with her hands before her eyes, in the utmost grief at having invaded the sanctity of the relic by her profane gaze. The last request they made, before C—— left Napier, was as follows: "Take it, show it to Queen Victoria, and bring it back safely to us." A higher compliment to a man could not be paid than entrusting him with this precious charge, with no acknowledgment beyond his word. It would be just as if the Emperor of Russia gave me his "blue diamond" to show my friends in England.

But, leaving these indoor sights as a resource for a rainy day, let us wander through the maze of wonders outside, while the Kawau wears its brightest autumn garb.

First in order comes the garden. There you find bushes of scented daphne growing with wild luxuriance, and a profusion of blossom that I have never seen equalled elsewhere; trees of geranium and heliotrope; English violets breathing forth their modest fragrance in retired nooks, and blushing beds of the ever-welcome rose. Gigantic aloes guard the corners of the walks, whilst on the hill-side is a dense jungle, or undergrowth of wild ginger, interspersed with a Japanese plant, from the pulp of which the exquisite rice-paper of commerce is made.

The india-rubber trees, tea and coffee plants, small date-palms grow side by side, and the only rule which prevents the garden becoming a small epitome of the vegetable universe, is that Sir G. Grey will not introduce any plant which requires artificial heat or cannot thrive naturally in the New Zealand climate. I think the list of fruit-trees in itself is enough to attract emigrants to a country of such wonderful capabilities.

In the early morning, before the sun had dried the cool dew off the ground, you could saunter out and begin your day with fruit; the only true way to enjoy it thoroughly being to pick it yourself when fresh. On one side ran a line of bushes, studded with the small purple guava whose flavour is a delicious acid, interspersed with ruddy pomegranates, which do not ripen quite so well as the oranges hard by. On the other side of the walk were citrons, lemons, large fig-trees, prickly pears from Malta, strawberries, and grapes, an enticing medley suited to the most capricious tastes.

In the single class of pines and firs, this little island is " Californiâ ipsâ Californior"; nearly every kind you can mention is there, though naturally they will not rival the American "big trees" in size for centuries to come.

But I am afraid of making this account too much of a catalogue; so we will proceed with our explorations. Every bay or head-land in the Kawau appears to be devoted to a different kind of animal. Close to the house, and on the point round which the mail-boats came, I saw some tree-wallaby from New Guinea. The "wallaby," let me say for the information of home readers, is a smaller variety of the kangaroo; but to most Australians even, my saying that I had seen wallaby perched in trees, like 'possums or monkeys, would seem as absurd as the story of Mark Twain's buffalo in *Roughing It*, where there is a picture of the horned and hoofed beast climbing after a hunter, who is perched in the top branches of a large oak. New Guinea is still a *terra incognita* to most of the world; and tree-wallaby are as little known yet, as black swans were on the first discovery of Australia. They are of a dark glossy brown, with rather lighter fur in front; and, as far as I could see, made no use at all of their tails for holding on, but kept them for the same object as a kangaroo,—to give an additional spring to their long hind legs. It is rather hard to find them, as they are extremely shy and acute of hearing.

On the next point are rock-wallaby, who live on the face of precipitous cliffs, and burrow like rabbits. Behind them, on the high plateaux, are the "forester" or "bush" kangaroo. I saw one "old man," standing away on the sky-line, who must have measured full six feet in height. The meadows near the house, and all the open ground is alive with pheasants, and coveys of the pretty little California quail with their black crests, who always keep a sentry perched on the stump of a neighbouring tree to give them timely warning of the approach of strangers. Towards the head of the middle harbour there is a colony of wild pea-fowl, which it seems sacrilege to shoot. We took no dog with us to hunt for them, but the sharp eyes of our guide quickly detected the brilliant plumage on the head of a fine old cock, glancing through the fern. You must shoot them running if they wont rise; but in either case it would be nearly as bad to miss them as a haystack. As we walked over the hills, I was glad to see English daisies and buttercups springing up on the soft turf; it made the place feel homelike and friendly. Little things of this kind are very powerful in recalling to one's memory the happy past; in the words of Wordsworth:

> "To me the humblest flower that grows can give
> Thoughts that do lie too deep for human tears."

I remember how we treasured some cowslip seeds, which I planted lately on the river-bank beneath our flax mill; they came from a dear old house in England, where every winter a small army of cousins used to meet for the Christmas festivities. Talking of Christmas, we have a mistletoe in New Zealand, but such an apology for the genuine thing; it is a much darker green, and has none of the shining white berries which make the home plant look so gay. It is wonderful how slight associations like these help to cement the link that binds us with such an intense clinging to the old country; the sight of a robin red-breast, the song of a thrush in a far-off land, like the face of old friends, awaken lively feelings of gratitude to the Acclimatization Societies. Colonial-born children soon get accustomed to decorating the house or church with rata, or tree-fern, or cabbage-tree; but to an emigrant these innovations never will seem so appropriate as the bright holly with its red berries, or the misletoe and ivy, which make our Christmas bush at home.

Nature must have made the Kawau with a special view to pic-nics and *al fresco* luncheons; for, choose what direction you will for your mid-day saunter, the only provision you need make for a meal is a small hammer to knock the oysters off the rocks, wherever you like to sit down on the shore. These rock-oysters are very small, but deliciously flavoured; they are not the same symmetrical shape as those at home, and therefore you find it easier to open them by a sharp blow on the butt with a stone or hammer, insead of using a knife to prise them. The natives bring great quantities into Auckland from the islands about here; and I found that, on board the steamer returning to San Francisco, some kits of oysters, which had lain in the full blaze of a tropical sun for more than a week, without receiving more than an occasional douche of salt water, were as fresh as when we started, which is a decided point in their favour.

You remember the saying in the Western States, that in the prairie-dog cities on the plains, you always find a "dog," an owl, and a rattlesnake living amicably in one hole. Well! in almost every bend of the Kawau, you will find an oyster-bed, a pair of Cape geese, and a small cottage at the head of the bay for some of the labourers. These Cape geese are strangely exclusive birds; they do not congregate in flocks, but seem to prefer a Darby and Joan existence, a perpetual *tête-à-tête*, and attack fiercely any intruders on their special domain. I do not think they ever leave the piece of water which they have first appropriated to themselves at the commencement of their wedded life.

At present there are about forty souls or eight families living on the island. To each is allotted sufficient ground for a small garden, a comfortable cottage, and as much firewood as they can use. In return for this and their wages, they are employed on road-works, clearing bush, planting, and other out-door works. I believe Sir George Grey intends to increase the number of inhabitants gradually to about two hundred; and he tells me that the only and most severe punishment he inflicts is banishment from the Kawau, which I should suppose is regarded much in the same light as the driving our progenitors Adam and Eve from the Garden of Eden after the fall. He enforces strictly temperance regulations; no one is allowed to import spirits or beer into the island except for medical purposes; but I believe the use of tobacco is freely permitted. At places in America, where I found the same rule, such as the Mormon Territory and "Shaker" Settlements, the people seemed none the worse for total abstention. Another scheme, which I sincerely hope he will carry out, is the building of villas for sea-bathing which would make a kind of sanatorium for people from Auckland during the summer months; they would be a special boon to invalids.

I should be sorry however to see the Kawau over-run at all by tourists, or becoming too busy a centre of industry, which would destroy its great charm of retirement. And yet the island is naturally very rich in resources for the money-making man. First, there is the great copper-mine, which is now lying perfectly idle; and secondly, I am nearly sure there is gold; for one day, I walked up a little bye-path to a water-fall, the basin of which and the surrounding rocks were quartz-reefs, and I believe the "colour" (of gold) has actually been seen there.

There is just a trifle too much excitement for me in wandering through the back-parts of this island, especially if you are accompanied by a dog. The latter is sure to go sniffing about in the bush by the side of the road, after wild pigs or cattle, and suddenly you hear a loud crackling of twigs, as the animals take to their heels; or should it prove to be an old bull in the thicket, the first you know of it is a sullen roar, which ("discretion being the better part of valour,") strongly tempts you to look for the nearest available tree. Away on the sky-line, a wild bull, with his ears erect, and lashing his tail as he scents the approach of man, may be and is a very fine sight; "but distance lends enchantment to the view," and, as I had been carefully impressed with the fact that, "when the dog sets them, you must be cautious, for they always come at the man and not the dog," I inwardly anathematized the brute of a dog at times. He invariably seemed to come upon a "lurking foe," at some awkward turn in the road where there was no tree with sufficiently low branches to climb, or where an open space left ample room for you to be caught in flight.

Seriously however I did hear of several narrow escapes from the cattle. Sir George Grey himself was attacked by a cow one day, when taking a photographer round the island to view the scenery. I forget who was the first object of his fury, but the unhappy photographer tumbled backwards into a hole about three feet deep, which concealed him from view, while Sir George stepped aside from the path just as she made her rush, coming off luckily with no worse than a slight tear in his clothing from one of her horns. Anyhow, the nuisance has become so great that some men are now constantly employed in killing them and salting down the beef for market. They make very slow progress however, in their work of destruction, and the cattle will continue to afford a sensation to future visitors for many a year to come. It is said, that sometimes mistakes are made between them and the domestic beasts on the farms. In one case, some sailors belonging to one of Her Majesty's men-of-war, which had put in here for a day or two, were allowed to land and go in search of sport after the wild cattle. All they succeeded in bagging was a valuable bullock, which was peaceably grazing near the house; "unconscious of his doom the little victim played." The second story was more laughable still, and "no harm done.". A couple of "new hands," or fresh arrivals from the old country, who were bidden to the chase, are said to have seen a beast approaching them, and took to trees with the utmost alertness. There they sat perched for hours, while the savage and unrelenting foe paced beneath them like a sentinel. Unfortunately as they thought at the time, they had dropped their guns and could not finish him off; so they remained like "patience on a monument" for some hours, until messengers arrived from the house in search of the missing men, and informed them that their *bête noir* was a tame bullock which had been frightened by the wild cattle, and taken refuge under the tree in which they were imprisoned. I trust I may be pardoned for repeating this oft-told tale, but as I mention no names and should probably have done exactly the same thing myself, perhaps no apology is needed.

Very many of the birds and animals which have turned out in the Kawau are seldom seen; but I saw the tracks of elk, Virginia spotted deer, fallow-deer, and other creatures. One rare species of bird is the Australian bush turkey, which must equal the capercailzie in size.

From where you look out towards the Coromandel Ranges and the Thames, there is a small head-land, where the wingless kiwi is carefully preserved. They are very scarce, and the feathers are much prized for making caps and cloaks among the Maories. It always appears to me a great pity when any birds or plant is destroyed before the approach of civilization. Man's works can generally be renewed, but in nature, a single species once extinct is lost for ever.

I am not prepared to argue that the dodo of the Mauritius, for instance, was a particularly graceful bird, or calculated to adorn the society in which it moved; but it was at least interesting for its very awkwardness; and what would our life be without the charm of variety. The little kiwi, of which one sometimes sees specimens for sale in Auckland, is a mottled-brown in colour, with a very long beak, like a hoo-poe; its legs look as if they had been stuck in, where the tail ought to be. On Darwinian grounds, it is possible to argue that these birds gradually "dropped" the fashion of wings, because there was no need to fly in islands where there is no quadruped larger than a rat to molest them. But, then, what of the gigantic Moa, whose fossil remains show him to have stood at least "twelve feet high in his stockings." With or without wings, he would have been a match for any beast of prey on earth; so that, after all, it seems best to suppose that they never had any such appendages, or simply gave them up for conveniency's sake, having no desire to leave their mother-country for foreign climates.

Quot homines, tot sententiæ! One lives and learns out here things that are passing strange. For example, I was told in Napier the other day, that nothing in the world improved land so much as to sow Scotch thistles on it broad-cast. "Horses and other stock are very fond of "the pink flowers; and after three years, during which the "roots have opened and manured the soil, the plant dies "down for want of its proper subsistence, and never re-appears." Do the burs never stick in the wool of the sheep all this while, and destroy its value? Fancy, spinning such yarns as these to the men who passed the thistle act in Victoria! There, in the month of November, before the seeds begin to fly through the air on their mischievous errand, a procession starts from each "station," armed with scythe and flags, to mark out the ground for cutting down the foe. The ceremony equals our harvest-home in importance; and if omitted, the neglect of it would be severely punished by law. I am not surprised that the owner of the Kawau was annoyed at finding a rank luxuriance of thistles sown here during his absence in England to prove this theory, for they show no signs yet of the dying down process. We shall be told next of a new and excellent substitute for tobacco; for, in the early days of the colony, the white traders did not scruple to sell dock-seeds to the simple Maories, which have taken only too strong a hold of the land on which they raised their tobacco-crops. Talk of giving "stones for bread!"; that would be a far less harmful act.

From the highest point of the Kawau, a magnificent view is to be obtained. On a clear day, Auckland is distinctly visible; whilst on the ocean side, you see the Great and Little Barriers, the Hen and Chickens, and all the other islands dotted about the entrance to the Hauraki Gulf. More immediately beneath you are the windings of Kawau Middle Harbour, which possesses all the charms of lake scenery in its stillness, with the addition of bright green salt water, over which you see the penguins swooping down with shrill cries on the shoals of fish. The island combines the park-like undulations of Blenheim, the bold cliffs and tides of Menai Straits, and the wooded mountain-sides of Killarney or the Trossachs.

But with all these delights, I think I enjoyed my last day most of all. We went out "stingareeing," or spearing sting-rays, a sport of which Dr. Kingsley gave such a vivid account in the *Field* about a year ago. I had been over in the morning to Rabbit Island; and while B—— landed with the gun, I was sitting in the boat and looking down into the clear depths below. Suddenly, there glided into the shallow waters three black monsters, floating slowly along, like dark clouds or shadows, at the bottom of the sea. They were "sting-rays," flat, circular, slimy masses, with malicious deep-set red eyes gazing upwards, and a long spike behind which first showed me where their tail began and head ended, covering the barbed sting with which they disable their victims. I tied my sheath-knife to the end of the boat-hook, and drove it into one of them, but I might as well have tried to hold an elephant with a skein of wool; the loathsome brute wriggled away from me and came to the top with a plunge, skating off along the surface, like the "ducks-and-drakes" which school-boys make with flat pebbles. The strength of the creature rather surprised me, and on my companion's return we "concluded" to make better preparations for an attack on them in the afternoon. Accordingly, after dinner, we got the right sort of weapon, which is a trident on a long pole, and fastened to a line. Fortune favoured us; the day was a little overcast, and there was not a ripple on the water to disturb it, so that I could see some way ahead, as I peered over the bows of the dingy, with the "grains," or spear, poised in my hand, and a few coils of rope ready to let out if I struck anything. The "sculler" also sits with his face the way he is going, so that he can steer better, and not frighten the fish by splashing his oars as he approaches. For a good half-hour we floated along the shore of the island, without securing more than a good-sized mullet, which would not have succumbed so readily, but for being stranded in a little pool by the ebb of tide. We exchanged places at last, and in five minutes or less I saw one of mine enemies slipping lazily over the rocks, while the receding waves sung a lullaby to his last comfortable doze. Slowly and silently we crept up, until we were well over him, then down B—— drove the grains into his ugly carcass. Off we went like lightning for a few yards, myself "holding water" as hard as I could. He at last came to a dead stop, and sulked at the bottom, until we fixed the "grains" more securely in his flesh. Then we had a royal struggle for the mastery, he trying to take us into deeper water, we hauling him up to the shallows, where he had less room to fight. At last we pushed him by main force into two feet of water, and, jumping out of the boat, I chopped off his ugly head with my tomahawk. I didn't quite relish the way in which he lashed his tail about in close proximity to my naked feet, for they say the sting is hard enough to penetrate even a thick leather boot. We lifted the inanimate mass into the boat, and as we rowed leisurely homewards cut out his barbed sting of ivory, about nine inches long, leaving the rest of his body for garden manure, for which it is very useful.

Next morning, as we were starting off again to spear "stingarees," we heard the distant pit-a-pat of the steamer's paddles, and in a few hours the *Comerang* had landed us in Auckland, to exchange the realities of everyday life for the pleasures of the dream-land we had left behind us.

THE NEW OVERLAND ROUTE, OR HOW TO GET TO NEW ZEALAND.

Now that the tide of emigration and travel has fairly set towards New Zealand, and she has entered upon a career of prosperity even greater than her best friends could have expected, it may be worth while to give people some idea of how the journey is to be made from England to the Antipodes. There are, at present, four distinct routes, all of which have excellences of their own to offer in different respects. The first and cheapest is to start by sailing-vessel direct from Glasgow, Liverpool, or London, the voyage by which takes about one hundred days. If you have a quantity of luggage, and if you are transporting to the new home all your Lares and Penates, such as furniture, stock-in-trade of farming implements or machinery, there is little doubt you would choose this route, as there is no tranship-ment to be undergone; and what you lose in time you gain in economy, for a first-class cabin passage only costs about £60; and assisted passages, which are now being granted by the Colonial Government at their London Agency, can be obtained for a sum varying between £8 and £2 for married people and single men, whilst unmarried women between 14 and 35 years of age are taken gratis. It is even said that a premium will soon be offered to heads of families, taking out two or three suitable girls to the Colony under their charge. There is an extraordinary demand at present for this class of labour—female domestic servants; a ship load of forty Norwegian girls, who landed at Napier lately, and none of whom could speak English with any facility, were all engaged the first day they went on shore; and in Auckland, when an emigrant ship is signalled, you will see in the office a list of perhaps two hundred names of people wanting servants; they have to wait their turn, and take whoever they can get when the ship arrives. Even then many are disappointed, and have to wait for another lot. The country is quite a Paradise for labour; for not only are wages high and hours short, but in social position servants gain so much, as they have a change of bettering themselves indefinitely here. And then a little experience in service goes such a long way; "it is easy to be a whale among minnows," and we have often to put up with pretentious ignorance, and teach our minnows what little they do know before they become "whales."

Another very favourite route for invalids, or men with large families, is to travel by the *Great Britain* from Liverpool, or one of Money Wigram's steamers from London, transhipping once only at Melbourne, from whence there is good communication every week with all parts of New Zealand. This voyage takes about sixty days to Melbourne, and eight days to Dunedin or Auckland. It has the recommendation of good English food all the way, and little trouble.

The third and most luxurious route perhaps, is to take the Peninsular and Oriental boat from Southampton, Venice, or Brindisi; the accommodation on board in the way of baths, berths, food, wine, piano, smoking-room, &c., is proverbially excellent, and the journey fairly interesting, if one has never seen Egypt, or Point of Galle before; but there is one great drawback to it in the passage of the Red Sea, which is at all times unpleasant, and frequently almost intolerable.

Last of all comes the New Overland Route by steamer, from Liverpool to New York, across America by rail to

San Francisco, and thence by steamer touching at the Sandwich and Navigator Islands to Auckland. In point of time (if the steamers on the Pacific were at all up to the mark) this would be incomparably the shortest way, and ought not to occupy more than six weeks; but, as a matter of fact, the journey is rarely accomplished under two months; and though there is much to see *en route*, the discomfort and positive danger of the American mailboats, and the constant delays in winter from snow-drifts when crossing the Continent, are gradually driving people away from what should be the high-road to the Southern hemisphere under more favourable circumstances. In any case it is better to return from than to go to New Zealand this way; as in coming home you are sure to find a steamer waiting for you any day of the week at New York, to put you "over the ferry," and can thus please yourself how long you remain at each place on the line of rail, without being tied to a day or two; whereas, going to New Zealand, you must be at San Francisco on a certain date to catch the mailboat, which only leaves once a month. I have tried it myself in both directions, and in giving a short account of it, prefer to describe my journey from Auckland homewards, so that I may have a double experience to guide me in recording my impressions. When I went out to New Zealand in 1871, there were two rival lines of steamers on the Pacific; the one ran from San Francisco to Sydney, *viâ* Honolulu and the Fijis; the other direct to Auckland, *viâ* Honolulu and the Navigators. The boats of the first were rather small but clean, and the table was liberally supplied with English cookery, viz., joints, puddings, and fruits. An American of the name of Hall had chartered the steamers *Wonga-Wonga* and *City of Melbourne*, from the Australian Steam Navigation Company; but there was not room for opposition, and he had to succumb to the superior capital and pretensions of his countryman Mr. Webb, to whom our extravagant little Colony, under Mr. Vogel's auspices, has been paying an annual subsidy of £60,000 for an ill-performed and uncertain four-weekly service. The steamers to which the safety (?) of Her Majesty's subjects and mails were recently entrusted, are three in number, the *Nevada*, *Nebraska*, and *Dacota*; great big wooden paddle-boats of 3,000 tons, with massive beam-engines, and enormous hulls. It has always been a moot point, what would become of them if their machinery broke down, as they do not carry sufficient sail to make steerage-way in case of any such accident; but passengers were always assured that there was no instance on record of bad weather or hard work affecting their powers of going; so on they went, in a reckless kind of way, till now we read in a recent number of the *Times*:—"On the arrival of the *Nevada*, in Auckland, on December 16th, a unanimous protest was signed by her passengers, against the state of the vessel; they were never twenty-four hours without one of the boilers giving out; for a considerable time the engines were altogether stopped, and the steamer lay for hours in the trough of a heavy sea, all hands, passengers and crew, working at the pumps by relays," &c., &c.

So much for the general history of the line; my personal reminiscences are nearly as unpleasant in many respects. For various reasons, my brother and I had kept deferring the day of our departure from month to month, until at last we had almost decided to leave Auckland by the *Nebraska*, in August, 1872. Shortly after she had left the harbour, in June, however, a sinister rumour began to spread abroad that she had brought small-pox down with her on the last trip from the United States, and that two of the seamen on board were infected when the vessel left Auckland again. Credence was attached to this report from the fact that a man named Thompson, who had been landed there sick, died shortly afterwards in hospital. There was a small panic in the island; New South Wales and Victoria quarantined our vessels; an enterprising doctor paraded a calf before his door in Parnell, whilst hundreds rushed to be vaccinated; and one read an advertisement in the papers about "a fresh heifer ready by the end of the month;" whilst opinions were freely expressed that the scourge would more than decimate the population if it were allowed to spread; and as for Maories, there would be no more need for volunteers or armed constabulary to protect us against the infinitesimal remnant of natives which would survive the infection. However, not more than four white people died; and the Thames chiefs prudently issued orders forbidding their people to come into town till the panic subsided. To our surprise we found that the natives were as fully alive to the merits of vaccination as ourselves, and had for some time had their own practitioners in the art. But nevertheless, we made up our minds that the *Nebraska* would not come back, and so we hurried our preparations to go by the *Nevada* in July. When she arrived, to our dismay we found her boilers sadly out of order, and the shaft on the port side suspiciously cracked in three places. "Small-pox or shipwreck," *utrum horum mavis, accipe*! We were on the horns of a dilemma, but decided to risk the latter evil, as Nancarrow, the Government inspector, said that she would be safe enough at half-speed, and with only eleven pounds' pressure of steam; but he urged that she should be laid up at the end of her voyage for repairs. She had then run over fifty thousand miles in sixteen months, without an overhaul; whereas (to show the difference) the Cunard and other first-rate boats are carefully examined each time they come into the dock at Liverpool. This was in July, 1872, and the *Nevada* has been running ever since, under protest from the captain, until her last mishap, as above, in December of the same year. Many of our fellow-passengers backed out at the last moment from fear of accident, but we came through safely enough after all. But I should be sorry to speak no good word for the line; although the stewards are extremely dirty and rather uppish, although the discipline is lax, and the officers do not look so neat as are those on Red Sea boats, with their spruce uniforms and (on occasions) white kid gloves, still there is a magnificent promenade along the whole length of the hurricane deck, from bow to stern, and the three tiers of cabins are wonderfully well ventilated, with the exception of an occasional whiff from the cattle, sheep, and poultry forward, which might be the case on any boat, where the meat is not stored in an ice-house. The cookery is questionable; there is an attempt at reform from the profusion of little dishes to which one is accustomed in an American hotel; but they have fallen between two stools in the effort, and there is a smack of both nationalities, with the distinctive merits of neither. Up to the end of the solids all goes smoothly; then pudding, cheese, dessert, and coffee are huddled on together to save time, and to prevent the meat growing cold for the stewards, who dine at the same table immediately after the saloon passengers have finished. The Englishman's love for a matutinal tumby is beginning to be understood, though at first the captain of the *Nebraska* could not understand "the Britishers wanting more water in the bath-room than would *wet their sponges.*" Beyond and above all this there is a barber's shop on board, which is not yet fully appreciated by us as it should be; all good Americans go to be shaven every morning, and seldom perform the office for themselves. To those who have never experienced the skill of negro barbers, hairdressing is robbed of half its pleasures; for all through the United States there are three occupations or professions almost monopolised by our black brethren, viz., barbering, waiting at table, and whitewashing houses.

In about three days' steaming from Auckland, one is out of the region of variable winds and into the tropics, where for the rest of the voyage a deliciously cool trade-wind blows steadily from the east, and prevents the heat from ever becoming oppressive. The "social hall," at the head of the cabin stairs, is a good sized comfortable room for reading in; piano there was none, but we soon found a couple of concertinas on board, and inaugurated "The Amateur Musical and Dramatic Club," with a dozen performing members. I contributed a collection of Orpheus Glees, Musical Times, and Mendelssohn's Open-air Quartettes, which our choir rendered very effectively. My brother performed on the Picco-pipe, and gave a few humorous recitations from Hans Breitman's famous ballads; and an old gentleman, called Donaldson, gave us some of the best comic songs I ever heard, one being "Kate McClusky, or the Gooseless Gander," the other an entirely new version of "Old King Cole," one verse of which might have been written to describe King Thakombau of the Fiji Islands, so accurate is the likeness. It was as follows:

> "His sign for Rex was a single X,
> And his drink was ditto double;
> So to read and to write were useless quite,
> And it saved him a vast deal of trouble."

The German consul from Hobarton, Tasmania, was our conductor, and to him we owed most of our success.

On the eighth day, at dusk, we sighted Upola, one of the Samoan or Navigator Group, and about nine o'clock p.m. we stopped off Pango-pango (the finest harbour in the South Pacific), until the canoes came out with a chance passenger or two, and a welcome supply of bananas, cocoa-nuts, and other fruits. I had heard that cakes of scented soap were much prized by these savages, and accordingly I had laid in a stock to barter for curios. I exchanged some with a gigantic chief who came on board, for a handful of the lovely green opercula shells, which make very neat sleeve-links or solitaires; but, to my horror and amusement, he raised it to his mouth, and, exclaiming interrogatively "kai-kai?" (food?) was going to make a bite at it, if I had not stopped him and explained its uses.

These Samoans are the most lovely race of savages with whom it has been my fortune to meet; they have not the flat noses, thick lips, and frizzled hair of the negro type, but have distinctly European features, and a very pleasing expression. The colour of their skin is a rich golden; their whole costume is limited to a light fringe of grass round the waist, and the women confine themselves in the way of tattooing to a couple of thin blue lines across the lips. The men are of great physical strength and enormous stature; they have a queer disdain for us whites, and say that while we employ brute force, *e. g.* Armstrong guns, etc., like a bull, they have the reason and intellect of the child who runs away from the bull.

They live a happy graceless life; the earth unasked produces her treasures in abundance; they have no need to dig when all is ready to their hand. They bask in the sunshine, or bathe in the cool waters of some retired cove, and cannot understand why we should come to thrust our business worries upon them, to buy their land and grow cotton and sugar, and disfigure the romantic picturesqueness of their islands with convenient but intrusive roads; and, above all, why we should send missionaries, who can't agree among themselves, and who attempt to introduce all-concealing garments, of which the want was before unknown. It isn't half as pretty a dress as the garlands of fresh flowers with which they love to adorn themselves in their artless and primitive simplicity. They are not moral, according to our ideas — far from it, but they have a strong sense of the æsthetic, and chastity does not rank as a virtue among them, where the reverse is no sin. · They are very clever at hammering out shillings into rude silver rings between a couple of stones, and they also bring for sale little tortoise-shell ornaments, inlaid with silver. Their coiffure might have come from Paris or London, for when I was there bright red hair was in vogue with both sexes. They plaster their heads over with lime for a few days, which destroys the original colour of the hair, and produces a loud saffron tinge. When a man becomes engaged, the fair *fiancée* often clips her flowing locks, and brings them to her Adonis, who plaits them in elaborately with his own, producing a most elaborate head-dress. The disgusting way in which they prepare kava, an intoxicating drink, by chewing, has often been described, and I do not care to repeat it.

Strangely enough, the Samoans are just one day behind all the rest of the world. Their Sunday should be the same day as in New Zealand and Australia, but, as their missionaries came from the East to them, and forgot to miss out a day in their reckoning, they have perpetuated the mistake. It was Monday on board the *Nevada* when we touched at Pango-pango, but with them it was still the Sabbath, and in consequence we were unable to "trade" to any large extent. In this respect, the missionaries have certainly produced the most stringent observance of their teaching, however much they may fail in checking immorality. I was the more struck with it, because a ship doesn't call here every day, and they must have felt sorely tempted to make the most of our visit by a little contraband dealing.

We heard a good deal about life in these islands from a lady who came on board here for San Francisco. She had been living in Apia, the largest of the group, for some time, and told us there were about fifty white settlers in all, British, German, and American. Her husband, an energetic Scotchman, who came to see her off, had taken up an immense block of land here for sugar and cotton, and his partner has lately been in England to try and form a Steamship Company for working the island trade, by taking Tahiti as a centre, and running boats thence to Sydney, Auckland, the Navigator and Sandwich Islands, and San Francisco. It seemed strange and somewhat incongruous, to see a highly-refined and well-dressed Englishwoman like Mrs. C—— step out of a canoe full of naked savages, and to hear her experiences of "roughing it." It shows what ladies can put up with in these out-of-the-way places, and what a curiously abnormal life some of our fellow countrymen lead out of England. Mrs. C—— was born in Tahiti, had been living in Sydney, Melbourne, had often visited New Zealand, and now after a few years in the Navigators, was going to California to see her daughter and nieces educated. I kept wondering to myself, how one that had never seen England could be so thoroughly English, and, in that lonely spot still preserve the fascination of manner which made her so universal a favourite on board our steamer. For the last eight years with one short interval, a sanguinary war has been going on in these islands between the young king and an usurping uncle. The natives have run very short of ammunition now, and were firing old bottles and all kinds of rubbish from their guns, with as much danger to themselves as their adversaries. Like the Maories, they never spare a wounded man; nay, worse, if your friends see you lying on the ground crippled, they decapitate you themselves, to save your relations and you the indignity of having your head exhibited to the women in the enemy's camp. The heads, however, when taken as trophies are only kept for a time, and then "returned with care" to their belongings to be buried with the body. Both sides seem to respect the white people, possibly from the fact of there being several men-of-war in harbour to protect their respective nationalities. When a European wishes to pass between the conflicting parties, he simply puts up his umbrella, which is the signal for "cease firing," while he walks over the neutral grounds in the middle of the two fortifications. We had two other passengers on board who contributed to our information on the subject. One a Frenchman, who was going to the States to raise capital, either for guano-islands or pearl-fisheries, I forget which. By the bye, the latter is just now the fashionable pursuit for our Colonial young ideas. "Fit up a small vessel with stores and defensive weapons, go off to North Australia to fish for pearls, and make your fortune in a couple of years." There is a smack of adventure, and at first sight an absence of steady grind, which makes the scheme sound attractive. The other gentleman, who knew Samoa, was our friend D——, a dry old Scotchman, the same who sang "Old King Cole" at our concert. He was quite a character, and to my mind spent a very happy life. He is an indefatigable naturalist, and had been wandering all over the Pacific Ocean, collecting new fishes, and birds, and insects, native weapons and implements, in fact, every kind of curiosity he could pick up. He told me that he has an estate in Southern Indiana, U.S.A., of miraculous beauty, on which there are seven or eight subterranean caves, equal if not superior to the celebrated Mammoth

Cave in Kentucky. He seemed to know all I could tell him, from my personal experience or hearsay, about the Kentucky Caves, the Caves at Deloraine in Tasmania, the Caves on the Blue Mountains of New South Wales, the Alabaster Cave at Folsom in California, or the Amber Caves near Rio Janeiro. So I caved in and let him do the talking. In the summer, he frequently has picnic parties of one hundred young ladies from Indianapolis and Cincinnati, to visit the wonders of his house and its vicinity. He has made the most beautiful pictures and designs of flowers, from the brightest feathers of birds, which he collected in different parts of the world. But his highest pride is in the fact, that he was the first man to tame humming birds; he prepares some honey and water for his pets, when he has a visitor, and places the liquid in a diminutive shell, giving it you to hold; and upon his whistling, two or three little "jets of liquid fire," (the ruby-breasted humming bird) dart down from the trees and sip from the shell in your hands. His only condition is that you must never touch or stroke the tiny things; it seems that *noli me tangere* is their motto, for they regard it as an unpardonable insult, and never return again if the rule be transgressed. Among other curiosities, he has the two-handled and two-edged sword, formerly used by the headsman of Saxony, which he bought after the last execution of that kind took place there. In his photograph-album there was an excellent cabinet likeness of Cakobau Rex of the Fijis, with the king's own mark X attached. This worthy monarch, when chatting to Mr. D——, among other reminiscences of his boyhood, told him that he distinctly remembered being taken out by his father for a walk before breakfast to select a meal; and that whenever he saw a particularly appetizing slave, his father gave the man orders to lie down on the ground, while the little lad

Thakombau battered his brains out with a toy-club. He has now taken to better practices; has acquired a gentlemanly taste for old Hollands, and formed a responsible government at Levuka of "mean whites," which is ignored by all the better class of settlers in his kingdom.

To return to the voyage proper. Shortly after leaving Pango-pango and the Samoan group, the *Nevada* began to exhibit refractory symptoms. Instead of running on an even keel, she became lop-sided and threw all the work on the port paddle-wheel, the shaft of which was known to be suspiciously cracked when we left Auckland. This was a mystery to us, especially as it made the pump in our bathroom on the starboard side incapable of use. But at last we discovered there was only too much reason for the step; it was a choice of two evils, for, although the shaft on one side was cracked, on the other side one-third of the crank had worn clean away; and it was a question whether at any moment we might not break down, and drift helplessly about, till at last possibly we should starve, or else be cast upon the New Hebrides or some unfriendly shore, to be knocked on the head by some cannibal like Thakombau, and eaten without even being properly cooked. I often started up from my sleep with the idea that the engines had stopped, and the bad times come; and one or two of us used to speculate as to whom we would eat first, if it came to a push. Our decision was babies first, and then the stoutest men, before they began to fall off and lose weight, which would cause waste. It really would be highly unpleasant for a vessel to break down in the Pacific; it is at present a vast deserted unknown ocean, considering its size; and except the sister-boat *Nebraska*, we had not sighted a sail the whole way. All our fears proved groundless, however, and we steamed into Honolulu safely enough in nineteen days from Auckland. The Sandwich Islands are an enchanting spot, as the ship glides into harbour with shoals of red, white, and blue flying-fish playing across the bows, skimming through the air, and dropping with a light splash into the clear depths below, where the white coral is easily seen, as you bend over the side. The town has a snug, bright appearance, nestled among cocoanuts and other rich tropical foliage. Cloud-capped mountains rise immediately behind it, clothed to the very tops with trees. The Kanakas or natives have such pleasing, good-natured faces, the men are strong, independent fellows, and the women have so free and graceful a gait, moving with their heads erect, and just sufficient swing in their walk to show the outline of their figures through their black or parti-coloured gowns, which have no waist or stays to spoil the general contour.

To adapt the words of Tom Moore—

> Lesbia wears a robe of gold,
>   But all so close the nymph has laced it;
> Not a charm of beauty's mould
>   Presumes to stay where nature placed it.
> Oh! my native gown for me,
>   That floats as wild as mountain breezes,
> Leaving every beauty free
>   To sink or swell as heaven pleases.

They add very much to their *tout ensemble* by wearing garlands of flowers, ferns, and everlastings round their necks and on their heads. On my last visit I was comfortably lodged by an old New England body from Vermont, at whose house I had a fine large room, with a shower-bath out in the garden; whilst I used to get my meals at the hospitable little British Club. This time, however, I found an enormous hotel built, in which the food is that of America, with the addition of an abundance of delicious fruits, whilst the verandah, and easy chairs, and natives standing below, rather reminds one of Shepheard's in Cairo. The steamers stop here a very short time; but Honolulu is already becoming a fashionable wintering-place, and we found the place full of our Transatlantic cousins, and some few passengers for the Antipodes. It is well worth stopping over here for a month to run down to Kilauea, the great volcano in Hawaii; the voyage itself is a short one, but as the mail-boat for San Francisco only passes once a month, few have so much leisure time to spare when running home on a hurried visit from the colonies. Besides, communication had been stopped between Oahu and the other islands at this time, owing to the small-pox, introduced into Honolulu by the *Nebraska*. We found she had not suffered as we expected during her last voyage hither, despite the infection on board when she left Auckland; but I believe she was heavily fined this time whilst in Honolulu, for having brought it to the island originally from San Francisco. We had time to ride up to the "Pali," a gap in the mountain-pass above the town, through which the trade-wind rushes, as through a funnel, with extraordinary force, and where one gets a fine view of half the island, including a precipice whence they used to throw their victims in former days, and Diamond Cove, where the beach is strewed with the white and bleaching bones of the warriors who fell in a great battle fought there by the victorious king Kamehameha I.

Half-way down, between the Pali and the town, where most of the European residents live, and thus escape the heat of the plain, we turned up a road which led to the American minister's house, and tethered our horses, whilst we had a swim in the pool below. I saw a Kanaka jump thirty feet down from an overhanging rock into this stream, feet foremost, and he seemed to think nothing of the feat. The only other ride for a passing visitor is down to the King's Palace in the Cocoanut Grove; and whilst there, I got a native to climb a tree and bring us down some green nuts. He tore the outer husk off with his teeth, getting a purchase on the nut with his feet and hands, like a monkey. The cool fresh milk, and the creamy coating inside, while still soft enough to be scooped out with a spoon, are proverbially delicious. The evening before we left, Madame Simonsen's Italian Opera Company gave a farewell performance at the little theatre; but the rival claims of the Royal Band, who are now rapidly improving, under the skilful tuition of a German master, drew away most of the islanders; they naturally prefer to encourage native talent, and then there is all the extra charm of sauntering about in the open air.

It is advisable, when stopping here, to lay in a stock of limes, pine-apples, bananas, and oranges for the voyage, as the supply on these American boats is very limited. The Chinese also make very cheap and comfortable cane armchairs, which are a great comfort on board.

The scene as the boat leaves Honolulu is rather interesting. Being the event of the month, all the rank and fashion of the place came to see us off. Queen Emma was there, in her neat little landau and pair, with the coachman and two footmen in dark green livery, and cockades on their hats. She is an universal favourite with both Kanakas and whites. I also noticed Prince William Lunalilo, a stout, goodhumoured-looking man, in pot-hat, white ducks, and cut-away black velvet coat. He has been elected king since I was there, on the death of Kamehameha V., and if he can only restrain his "mixed moral character," and curtail his liking for ardent spirits, there is no reason why he should discredit the throne from want of ability.

Our new steamer was the *Idaho*, the slowest old tub

that ever disgraced a mail-service. We took fifteen days to get to San Francisco, a voyage which I had made in eight-and-a-half days in the *Wonga-Wonga*. And the torments we endured from dirt, incivility, heat, and crowding! The anxiety of travelling by the broken-down *Nevada* was bad enough (and they sent her back to New Zealand again, in the face of a protest from her captain, instead of laying her up for repairs), but in the *Idaho* it was a case of "out of the frying-pan into the fire."

Once the line is fairly established, as it promises to be, the big steamers will be increased in number, and run right through between Auckland and San Francisco, thus avoiding the transhipment at Honolulu, and saving time; but on this occasion we had taken on board a much smaller steamer, not only our original complement, but fifty additional passengers from the Islands. I never slept below after the horrors of the first night, but coiled myself up in a 'possum rug on deck, where I awoke early enough every morning to get the "refresher" of a douche from the hose, when the sailors were washing the decks. And yet, every cloud has a silver lining. The officers were particularly pleasant. Captain Howell was a brother-in-law of Jeff. Davis, late President of the Confederate States; the purser, Mr. Howard, was a Harvard man, and therefore was especially civil to me when he found I was a brother to the man who led Oxford to victory against his fellow-collegians.

We managed to shake down somehow, though we were never exactly comfortable, and with the aid of some pretty half-castes from Honolulu, who have a particular talent for part-music, our concerts not only resumed their former prestige, but became less formal and more social.

I was rather disgusted at the extent to which gambling was carried in the smoking-room. There were several "old hands" from Ballarat gold-fields who were utterly reckless at unlimited loo and lansquenet. Frequently two or three hundred pounds changed hands in an evening, and it was with peculiar delight I learnt that Simonsen, the husband of the prima-donna before mentioned, dishonoured his I O U on reaching dry land, which punished the chief winner to some extent, as he held it.

Exactly five weeks after leaving New Zealand (ten days longer than we ought to have been), we steamed through the Golden Horn, which as usual was enveloped in a cloud of mist, into San Francisco Bay.

Now were I to commence a description of all that is to be seen in California, I might fill a book easily; but so much has already been written on the subject that I confine myself to merely mentioning what ought to be seen, and hinting at the agreeables or otherwise of the journey.

Of all the cities in the United States of America, San Francisco is best provided with hotels. There is not a pin to choose between the Occidental, Cosmopolitan, Grand, and Lick House.

During the two days in which the traveller ought to recruit his wasted energies for the overland route, by a generous diet and a comfortable bed to sleep in, he will be pestered by "railway touts," and the sooner he makes up his mind by which route he is to cross the Continent the quieter will be his life. This rigorous competition between the railways has a good effect in one way. They bid against each other in promoting one's comfort during what I think a most fatiguing journey. One offers to run a "through car" to Ogden, and thence to New York, with a single change at Omaha, if you can make up a small party. Another has a "compartment car," which secures you all the privacy of your own sitting-room, and enables ladies to dress and wash in comparative comfort, without sitting on their berth or standing in the public passage. By this line you get "hotel cars;" and by feeding while the train is running, you have time to stretch your legs when it stops, instead of bolting a hurried meal in the wayside restaurant; by that line you see Niagara Falls and the Hudson. Or you can branch off at Cheyenne, and go through Denver to Kansas city, if you are fond of buffalo hunting; on the Saline River, which may be reached from Fort Hays, you will get the best of sport about July or August, and the officers at these remote stations are only too glad to have an opportunity of showing their hospitality to a casual visitor. But the best plan is to take the journey as easily as possible, unless you care to make yourself a martyr. Don't rush across the Continent in seven days, as you *can* do; but before leaving the Pacific coast drive to the Seal Rock, where the sea-lions disport themselves; spend an evening at the Chinese Theatre, and another at Woodward's Gardens. Then devote three days to the Geysers. Go there *via* Healdsburg, across the Hog's Back, and return *via* Calistoga. If possible, get Foss or Albertson to drive you, and you will experience a genuine sensation. The scenery is lovely, but the roads are narrow and the hills steep. The horses have the good sense to keep in the middle of the road, but often there are very few inches between you and the precipice. The drivers are clever fellows and seldom have an accident, but they take a fiendish delight in shaving it close at times.

Having seen this much, you will now be ready for a fair start, as follows: Cheque your luggage through to Ogden (mail passengers are allowed 250 lbs. weight, or 150 lbs. in excess of ordinary travellers), and keep only a small valise with a change of linen and necessaries at hand. If you are adventurous enough to see everything thoroughly, leave the mail at Lathrop, and visit the Yosemite Valley, which is unrivalled in its wonders. After ascending four thousand feet of the Sierra Nevada, you travel into the valley by a precipitous path, and find yourself as it were in an enormous oblong box, with cliffs rising sheer up on all sides to a height of two thousand to three thousand feet. The features of the place are strangely varied and beautiful; waterfalls, lakes, magnificent pine trees, snow-clad mountains, and in the midst of all this wild nature at least two excellent inns. On the return journey, the best way is to strike the main line again at Galt, taking *en route* the Calaveras grove of " big trees" (*Sequoia Gigantea*, or as we erroneously call them, *Wellingtonia*).

But Australia, in this respect of " big trees," can hold her own against, and even surpass California; for in the Dandenong Ranges, near Victoria, white gum trees (*Eucalyptus Amygdalina*) have been recently discovered by Mr. Joseph Harris, of South Yarra Nurseries, Melbourne, which attain a height of 520 feet, or 40 feet greater than that of the tallest *Sequoia*. And I think the giants of the Antipodes are the more beautiful trees of the two; they are not so massive at the base, nor so like an enormous extinguisher in shape as the *Sequoia* with its insignificant branches, but they run up in a clean white spar for 300 feet, and then spread out into large leafy branches, more like those of the European forest trees. There is more symmetry about them than in the *Sequoia*, though possibly the latter from its girth contains the greater quantity of timber.

Half-way down the eastern side of the Sierra Nevada, it is worth breaking the journey for a day to visit Lakes Donner and Tahoe, about which Mark Twain has written so enthusiastically. The valley through which the drive to the latter lies is remarkable for the forests of enormous red pines, and the variegated rocks brilliant with iron, silver, and cinnabar ore. Lake Tahoe itself is surrounded by snow mountains; and the blue waters are so clear that you can see the trout a hundred feet below open their mouths and swallow your bait. They say all that sinks (man, beast or timber) never reaches the surface again, from the peculiar tenuity or lightness of the water.

At Emerald Bay I found an old British tar in charge of Mr. Holladay's cottage, about whom I annex a paragraph from one of the Californian papers:

"RUBICON POINT—EMERALD BAY.

"A few miles further down is Rubicon Point, celebrated from the fact that the shore there goes down almost perpendicularly, a depth of one thousand feet being almost immediately attained. The gem and crowning glory of Lake Tahoe is Emerald Bay, which is formed by a height in the lake and a break in the mountains. The water at the entrance of this nook is emerald green, hence the name of the bay. At the upper end of the bay, which is two miles from the lake, there is a neat cottage, the property of Ben. Holladay, jr. It is sheltered by a rocky bluff, which protection has several times saved the house from being swept into the lake by winter avalanches. The mountains above the house are very steep, and are forbidding in their sombre colours; in fact, the spot is at once the most Alpine and attractive that I have ever seen. There is a small island in the bay, which greatly adds to its beauty. The whole place looks like a painting of Alpine scenery, with an Alpine cottage and garden. "Old Dick," a venerable old sailor, takes care of the place for Holladay. His face is seamed and lined with the effects of the sun and weather. He comes around on elephantine and frozen feet, done up in grain sacks. His beard is frizzled and his breast exposed, and he has altogether the style, awkwardness, and innocence of a sailor of the days of Nelson. Holladay, it is seriously said, bought Dick with the bay. The old man has his self-made grave all ready, when the sound of the final eight bells warns him that his watch for time has ended, and that it is time for him to "turn in" to eternity. The greatest wonder about Dick lies in the fact that he has wintered at Emerald Bay for seven years. The winters here are six to seven months long, and blinding snow storms, wintry wails, the frost feathered forests, with the freezing and hush of the voice of running water, and the departure of the song birds, make the lake at that season an almost sepulchral place of residence, even where there is company. Dick keeps no human company in his lonely bay, save that of a large cat, the language of which he professes to understand, and she, he says in turn, can in her own wise way translate every word he utters. He has his chair, and the cat has hers; and they sit and crack yarns together on long winter nights when the wind is howling and when the snow is up to the roof of the house. Dick says he has seen sixteen feet of snow on the level at Emerald Bay. On one occasion a let up in the weather allowed Dick in his boat to revisit the world of half a dozen persons who winter here at Tahoe City. He went home with a cargo of whisky, not in his boat but in his stomach; and early night fell on the vast deserted lake while he was yet miles away from his home. It blew, and Dick in his alcoholic helplessness could not guide the boat, which capsized late in the night, throwing him into the freezing water. He clung to the bottom of the boat until soberness and morning returned, when he managed to right her and get home, but his feet—his "flukes" as he calls them—were both frozen, and all his care and skill in doctoring such an affliction have failed to completely restore the use of one of them, with which he goes stumping around. Dick would in outward appearance at least make an admirable Captain Cuttle. But his manner is too quiet and sedate for that tender and jovial old character. In fact, Dick appears to dream even in company, and while physically present seems to be mentally absent in his winter solitude on Emerald Bay. Dick has had several escapes from avalanches, one of which once roared down the mountain, and passed within ten feet of his door, sweeping rocks and pine trees like chips before it into the lake, and sending a tidal wave from the shore which would have swept a ship before it. It is worth a week's time and the cost of a trip here to see Dick and Emerald Bay alone."

And now, before we get to Utah, let me describe some of the experiences of a Pullman's Palace Car, which is erroneously supposed to obviate all the inconveniences of railway travel. It is a vast improvement on the ordinary carriage; but far, very far from perfection. Unless you have one or two agreeable friends, the journey and scenery are intensely dreary after leaving California, for at least a couple of days. When crossing the Alkali Plains in summer, the white impalpable dust which creeps through double windows and closed doors, inflames the eyes and cracks the lips; and you feel just as if you had a feverish cold. In winter you run a chance of getting snowed up in the drifts, while crossing the Rocky Mountains; and visions of salt junk and cracker for possibly some weeks do not enliven the prospect. If the cars are full, or if you have not the exceptional luck of securing a "compartment car," the company is rather mixed at bed-time; and if it proves embarrassing to a shy man, what must it be to the feelings of the fairer sex? I always felt puzzled how to act when put into a section, with some unprotected female in the lower berth; but at last I concluded that the best way was for me to scramble up to bed first and fasten the top part of the curtains, leaving the inmate beneath to retire when she liked. Of course the lady has to be up first and out of the way, or else she runs the risk of being trodden upon when the "top berth" steps down in the morning. There is more room for sleeping than on board ship (nearly double as much), but not so much for dressing and little or no privacy. It seemed to me that the basin, &c., at one end of the car ought to be devoted to ladies, and that at the other end to gentlemen; but even then it is more unpleasant than ludicrous at times to see some poor girl rush from one end to the other, and possibly find herself in the wrong box after all, among a lot of dirty begrimed beings of the male sex in extreme dishabille. One gets the smuts and grits, that fall through the ventilators, regularly ingrained into one's skin by morning, from rubbing against the pillow as the train vibrates. I was patiently waiting my turn at the washing-basin one morning, when suddenly I felt a sharp thump in the ribs from behind. I started and looked round, thinking some facetious person had done it for a joke, and would probably peep out again from his curtains; when a testy old gentleman next to me muttered "No need for you to watch my wife dressing, Sir." I apologised, and told him my reason for turning round to inspect the premises. The truth was, she had been sitting up in bed to dress, and from the limited space at her disposal had caught her elbow against me in the operation.

But there are more absurd *contretemps* than this. I had before noticed that American couples are rather demonstrative with their endearments in public, both on the "cars" and steam-boats; but this beat all.

In the "sections" of a railroad car, as in a wooden house, even whispered remarks are very audible, especially at night when everything is still. *Par exemple*, one evening, when we had retired, a low voice was suddenly heard from the centre of the car, "Fanny, Fanny, give me a kiss, and say you forgive me." Then, a little louder, "Fanny, Fanny, I can't sleep unless you say you forgive me; give me a kiss, and say you forgive me." At last, the voice of the conscience-stricken and penitent husband, regardless of the smothered tittering from the surrounding partitions, spoke again: "Fanny, Fanny, just one kiss, and say you forgive me!" until, at last, a peppery old Indian officer down at the end of the car popped his head out and shouted, "Oh, Fanny, for goodness' sake, *do* give him a kiss, and let us get some sleep!" Even then, amidst the outburst of laughter from the other passengers, you could hear the unhappy Caudle catching it in a curtain-lecture: "There! I told you so! Now you see what you 've done! I knew everyone could hear you!" But at last peace reigned, and possibly Fanny gave him the narcotic kiss of reconciliation for which he had been asking.

It is best, if with ladies, to provide little hand-basins for the journey, as they can then wash behind the curtains of their berth; and it would be prudent also to take a hamper of provisions to fall back on at odd times, as with a few bright exceptions, in the case of oases like Humboldt, the food is execrable—a repetition of coffee, tea, poisonous Bourbon whisky, ham and eggs, woodeny beefsteaks, and indigestible hot cakes. One thing alone are you always sure of getting good, and that is iced-milk. It may almost be called the national beverage of America.

After leaving the Alkali Plains, those who wish to spend a day in Salt Lake City had better take the steamer at Corinne, as they then see something of the inland sea itself, including a most interesting twenty miles down Bear River Creek, where the dead willows, killed by the steady encroachment of the salt water, afford a home to myriads of birds—pelicans, eagles, owls, black snipe, cranes, reedbirds, blackbirds, and balloon-birds, which prey on the river fish as they come to the surface, belly upwards, from the same cause which destroys the vegetation. At Lake Point, you can have a bathe in the lake, a sensation not unlike sitting in an easy chair, for you cannot sink, and can lie back and float without any effort to support the body.

A drive of twenty miles brings you to the home of Brigham Young. This city, in many ways, is very like Christ Church, New Zealand: the same background of hills, the houses hidden among orchards of English trees, the running water in the streets, and the orderly appearance of the people.

From this to Ogden by rail is about forty miles; and as the remaining sights henceforward do not strictly come under the head of The Overland Route, I merely enumerate my experiences going and returning. I chose the Pennsylvania Central for my westward journey, and thought the sight of the Alleghanies grander than anything I saw subsequently. While in Kentucky I visited the Mammoth Cave; the celebrated horse-breeding establishments in the Blue Grass country; and I also spent a day with the Shakers near Lexington, where I was so charmed with the quiet peaceful life they seem to lead at Pleasant Hill, that I nearly felt tempted to accept their invitation, and enter upon a novitiate of six months, to see whether I could make up my mind to stop. When returning home, I chose a more northern route, and passed through Chicago, which was then being "phœnixed," or rebuilt from the ruins of the great fire; probably the most gigantic building operation the world has ever known. After submitting for forty-eight hours to the impositions and annoyance of the "hackmen" at Niagara Falls, I gladly found myself in New York, and embarked on the famous Cunard s. s. "Cuba" for Liverpool. A delightful voyage of ten days, to the pleasure of which contributed the most genial of captains, the most seaworthy of boats, and the most liberal of diets (who would not remember the suppers of Welsh rarebits, devilled bones, grilled sardines, and roast oysters?), brought me safely home again.

P.S.— Since writing the above, the San Francisco mail-service to New Zealand has been discontinued. Had its promoters from the first established a regular and trustworthy service, the line could not fail to have paid; but they effectually cut their own throats, as I have described above, and the unfavourable reports sent all the passengers round the other way, *viâ* Brindisi. It will not, however, be long before New Zealand and New South Wales will secure a really efficient line on the Pacific; and steamers are now building for the purpose on the Clyde. Thus we shall see England monopolize this route as effectually as she has done that of the ocean steamers in the Atlantic and elsewhere.